Kenwick Drive
Growing up Italian in Lyncourt

Lugi Visconti

Field Days Press

www.FieldDaysPress.com

Field Days Press
www.FieldDaysPress.com

Cover Design: 2016 Maria De Angelis mariadeangelis.nyc

Kenwick Drive/ Lugi Visconti. -- 1st ed.
ISBN 978-0-9976245-0-2

For Little Pauly

CONTENTS

CHAPTER ONE

THE MOVE TO LYNCOURT

We broke Gramma's heart when we moved out of her upstairs apartment on Pond Street in the summer of 1965. Mom told her that two bedrooms weren't enough for a family of five. Our exodus from the North Side of Syracuse took us all of two miles to Kenwick Drive, in a foreign country called Lyncourt.

Why you a move so far away?

Gramma and Grampa DiVirgilio both emigrated from Italy in the early 1900s. The North Side was inhabited mostly by people right off the boat from Italy and Germany. Proud, working class people with strong beliefs in Church, family, and heritage filled the neighborhoods. Mom-and-Pop shops and businesses dotted the streets, maintained by a sense of loyalty between proprietors and customers alike. People took care of their meager possessions, and the surroundings were neat and clean.

Gramma Theresa came from the Giliberti family in Bari, Italy. They shortened their name to Gilbert after moving to America. While coming over on the boat she saw a banana for the first time. Upon eating part of the peel, she declared that she didn't like them. Gramma never came close to five feet in height, and she shrunk as she got older. She met and married my grandfather in Syracuse, New York, and lived the vast majority of her life in the same house on Pond Street.

The two-story, two family house provided extra income for the young couple, who hosted many gatherings in the clean, simple basement that included an additional stove and countertop for Gramma, a handmade bar for Grampa, and two long tables for their guests. Strings of colored Christmas lights stayed up all year round to impart a festive atmosphere, and vinyl records provided music for dancing. A separate room at the back of the basement housed a well-stocked pantry.

Gramma cooked massive amounts of food! She loved to bake, and became renowned for the variety of ornate and addictive Christmas cookies that she gave away to any and all. My cousins still laugh about the times Gramma visited their camp on Oneida Lake. She'd bring a main course, a side dish, and a dessert, and Grampa always brought a big watermelon. When departing she'd say, *Tanks for every ting*.

My grandfather and namesake, Louis, came from Italy by himself at the age of sixteen, followed several years later by his younger brother Nicholas. Another brother, Michael, set his sights on Australia. After leaving, all three brothers sent money back to the old country. Grampa worked at the local railroad for fifty years, and supplemented his income by selling Woodmen of the World insurance policies. In his spare time he participated in two local Italian clubs, The Sons of Italy and the Onesta e Lavoro lodge. Like many Italians, he made his own wine. I remember a small room in his basement that we called the wine cellar. I liked the smell of the old wine barrels and stealing a glimpse of the pocket-sized revolver stashed away in a cigar box at the back of one of the shelves. In another small basement room he kept his tools. He stored assorted nuts and bolts in empty bottles that screwed into lids nailed to the bottom of shelves or in the rafters. Empty cigar boxes contained the leftovers of his handyman work.

Everybody liked Grampa, but he died of cancer right before I made my first Communion. I always wished that he had lived longer and I had known him better.

The DiVirgilios' first child, Rosemary, arrived in 1931, followed three years later by a second daughter—my mother, Anne. Annie and Ro shared one of the two bedrooms in the first floor apartment. The girls both went to elementary school at Assumption Catholic Academy—at the end of Pond Street a few blocks away. Both were pretty girls and popular, too. Ro made the cheerleading squad but Annie didn't, because she wasn't too coordinated. The boys liked Annie better, though. She wasn't as domineering as her sister.

Ro never married—and by the time she reached middle age, she couldn't care less. Ro kept a full schedule with work, travel clubs, and the local Democratic Party. She had enough drama and aggravation from them to keep her happy, and chose not to include solving a man's problems in her agenda. Though she was physically attractive, her Type A personality likely worked against her when it came to potential suitors. Most men wanted wives who were content to stay at home—the idea of a female boss was not appealing to the typical Syracuse male.

My Dad, Leo Visconti, Sr., entered the world in 1933. He was the third of four children born to Sam and Agnes Visconti on the West Side of Syracuse. Dark-haired Sam came from Sicily and redheaded Agnes from Ireland— which made them, at that time, an interracial couple. Unbeknownst to Agnes, Sam kept busy cultivating other families around the state. A traveling salesman for the Electrolux Vacuum Cleaner Company, Sam found it hard to keep his hose where it belonged. He abandoned his West Side family, leaving Agnes unstable. My Uncle Joe and Aunt Mary pretty much raised their younger brothers, Leo and John.

I asked Dad how he met Mom, and he said it happened after he and his buddies raided a high school dance at another school. Gramma and Grampa tried to dissuade Mom from dating a half-Irish boy who came from the wrong side of town, but more than likely this just served to drive her into his waiting arms. Annie was a looker, and Leo fell hard. He took her to the parkway along Onondaga Lake to watch the submarine races, and married her at the tender age of 23, after serving his draft notice with the U.S. Army.

In 1955 Annie and Leo moved into the upstairs apartment at her parents' house on Pond Street. She felt right at home in the duplicate layout of her childhood home downstairs, with her family just a few steps away. Thrilled to finally have the bedroom to herself, Ro soon began to fill it with junk, a skill she perfected for the remainder of her life. After Ro and Gramma became the sole inhabitants of the first floor, she expanded her hoard to the basement, burying Gramma's other kitchen, the bar, the tables, even the dance floor under mountains of bric-a-brac. Poor Grampa probably rolled over in his grave.

Annie and Leo began to fill their second bedroom in 1957 with the birth of my sister Terry, named after Gramma. Leo, Jr. followed in 1958, and I made it three kids in one room in 1960. I'm named after Grampa Louis, but everybody called me Lugi – short for Luigi.

A blue collar guy to the core, Dad somehow began his career selling Metropolitan Life Insurance from an office in the State Tower Building in downtown Syracuse. Perhaps the idea of this livelihood had come from Grampa selling Woodmen of the World—I'm not really sure. His brief career in sales ended as soon as his brother Joe established a successful construction company, The Visconti Corporation. Dad found his true calling as a heavy machine operator. I always thought he looked a lot like Fred Flintstone.

When the population of the North Side outgrew the available housing during those prime Baby Boom years, it spilled over into the immediate outskirts of Lyncourt and Eastwood. Many of my friends from Lyncourt had also come from the North Side, making us neighbors twice. Everybody knew everybody in Lyncourt. You couldn't help it, because it's only a mile and a half long. Eastwood borders Lyncourt, and a natural rivalry developed, despite—or more likely encouraged by—common bloodlines. Most of my childhood friends were of Italian descent, their last names ending with a vowel—but this alone did not guarantee parental approval. Italians can be judgmental of other people... *especially* other Italians.

•••

It's getting crowded on Pond Street.

On moving day to Kenwick Drive, the Visconti kids are eight, six, and four. A little boy stands on our front lawn. He looks like he's waiting for us.

I'm Bobby, I'm almost four and I live right there, pointing two doors away.

I see a half-naked little boy in a diaper standing in Bobby's driveway. He's smiling at us.

Who's that kid in the diaper?

That's my brother Pauly.

What's wrong with his diaper?

He poops a lot.

In addition to Little Pauly, Bobby Vinciguerra's family includes older siblings David, Karen, Louie, and Patty. Bobby often comes over to sit and watch my Dad paint.

Mom tells Dad, *I think this little boy likes you, Leo!*

Mrs. Vinciguerra, the former Angela Tanzarella, went to Assumption Catholic with Mom and Aunt Ro.

Ro was Angie's bridesmaid when she married Louis Vinciguerra, Jr.

It's a small world.

Bobby becomes my first friend. He rings our back doorbell for me to come out. The front doorbell goes ding-dong and the back doorbell just goes ding. That's how you know which door to answer when the bell rings. Mom opens the kitchen window next to the back door and he sees her.

Mrs. Zooconti, can Lugi come out?

The Vinciguerras get to stay outside later than we do—including Little Pauly. It drives us nuts to hear them still playing outside after dark.

I say, *It's not fair, Mom, I'm older than Bobby and Pauly and they're still out.*

Leo says, *It's not fair, Mom, I'm in the same grade with David and you said I'm better behaved than him.*

Terry says, *It's not fair, Mom, why does Karen get to stay out later than me?*

Mom says for all of us to shut up unless we want to go to bed now, too. Then the doorbell goes ding, and it's Bobby at the back door again.

Mrs. Zooconti, can Lugi come out?

No! You go home and go to bed!

After making friends with the Vinciguerras, I meet the Savastanos, who live next door to us in the other direction. The Savastano family includes Susie, a year younger than me and a quiet girl, Nicky, three years my senior and a little crazy, and Joe, Kathy and Mary, all much older and therefore ignored. The Savastanos bear a dark Italian complexion. The kids at Lyncourt School call Nicky *Chief* and sometimes *Savage*. Nicky's natural gifts include speed, strength, and shortness of temper— so the kids only call him *Savage* from a safe distance. I like Nicky from the first day we meet, but some days I fear him, too. It would be dangerous to get him mad.

Not long after we move in, my brother Leo attracts the attention of the lady across the street by peeing on the side of our house. She screams, **You little animal!** Now we're on the growing list of unsuitable playmates for her boys, Tim and Gerry Gacioch. Mrs. Gacioch doesn't like the Vinciguerras' late curfew nor the look of Pauly's diaper, and she considers Nicky a little crazy and possibly dangerous. I don't know how I made her list, but it's my first lesson in guilt by association.

•••

The bungalow-style houses on Kenwick Drive have decent-sized yards for playing in, and trees and sidewalks give the street a homey feeling. Construction happened sporadically between 1920 and 1950, and our

30-year-old house stands adjacent to much younger neighbors. Our house has four bedrooms, which to us seems like a palace compared to Pond Street. I have to share a bedroom with Leo, but on the plus side we get the biggest room upstairs. Terry gets the other one to herself, and my parents sleep in the front bedroom on the first floor.

The galley kitchen has a window looking out to the backyard and a small table next to the refrigerator. We eat our meals together crammed in at the kitchen table. The dining room stands unused except for holidays or visits from relatives—mostly Gramma, Grampa, and Aunt Ro—but serves as the connector piece between the stairway going up and a small hallway leading to the only bathroom.

Our basement, which we call the cellar, functions mainly for laundry and storage, but like many Italian families', ours includes an auxiliary kitchen complete with an extra stove, old refrigerator, and an ancient table and chairs. The tiled floor in the cellar shows evidence of repeated sewer backups. For us kids, the best thing about the cellar is the attached garage that faces the backyard instead of the street. Three concrete steps at the end of our driveway remove any consideration of ever parking a car inside it. The rusted garage door seems to weigh a ton whenever you try to open it. Two tons when it slams shut on your big toe.

•••

Summer ends, and it's raining hard outside on the first day of school. I'm excited to start Kindergarten. Mom's frantic trying to get three kids ready for school. The back doorbell rings—it's Bobby. He's wearing a yellow raincoat with the hood folded up in front. He looks nautical out there in the elements. His rubber boots come up almost to his knees—all he needs is a fishing pole to complete the look. I'm smiling and waving at him from the window and he calls up to Mom, puddles of rain filling the fold in his hood.

Mrs. Zooconti, can Lugi come out?

No! He has to go to school. You go home!

My mother sends me to her alma mater, Assumption Catholic, which is two miles away on the North Side. All of the school-age Vinciguerra kids go there, along with Terry, Leo, and me. Since it's too far for us to walk, our parents take turns driving a crowded car pool. Seven kids in one car makes for familiar acquaintances. Every other kid on our end of Kenwick walks to Lyncourt School, the public school four blocks away. Most Catholic children in Lyncourt either go to nearby St. Daniel's School or they attend church school there. I tell Mom that I want to walk to Lyncourt School with the other kids, and I don't mind going to church school afterwards. She says that she wants her kids to go to the same school that she went to, so off to Assumption we go. Dad tells her that our new neighbors go to St. Daniel's, but she says Assumption is better than St. Daniel's.

That's not a real church.

Dad protests and Mom says, *Oh, what do you know?*

Grampa Vinciguerra sometimes drives us to school in the van he uses to run his little grocery store, a profitable business in the days before supermarkets arrived. We pile into his van and there's plenty of room so we're not sitting on top of each other like we do in the car. I like the mixed aromas of fresh produce, dairy, and butcher shop, and want to go with Grampa V. to his store and forget about school.

Little Pauly is too young for school but he likes to ride along. His Grampa calls him Smilin' Joe, and often gives in. Pauly stands next to the van in his pajamas and smiles at Grampa until he says, *Okay, Smilin' Joe, you get in, too.* Or until his Mom drags him back into the house in tears. Grampa V. drives us to school and puts a few extra miles on the van to bring Pauly back home. Both of them smile most of the way.

Mrs. Gruender teaches Kindergarten at Assumption. She's nice. The principal's office is across the hall, and you only go there if you're in trouble. I never hear any noise coming from the principal's office but I often see kids crying on their way out, sometimes even waiting to go in.

The girls all wear the same uniform, and it's a problem if they don't dress *exactly* like the other girls. Black shoes, white socks, and a button-up white shirt with a Peter Pan collar. A wool uniform skirt or jumper completes the look. The boys wear ties, mostly clip-ons, to look respectable. On class picture day they wear a suit jacket, too.

I'm a big boy now, almost five years old, and I tell Mom that I want to walk alone from school to Gramma's house. I don't need Gramma to hold my hand and walk me home from Kindergarten. It's only four blocks away, and straight up the street. I tell her that the other boys laugh at me.

But Italian mothers know how to play the guilt card, and Mom learned from a master.

Gramma loves you and you'll hurt her feelings. Don't you love your Grandmother?

Yes, but I don't want to walk with her.

You walk home with Gramma or I'll give you a good one.

Mom resorts to threats if the guilt card fails. After that, look out.

Mrs. Gruender dismisses Kindergarten the next day with Gramma nowhere in sight. I make it a block toward her house when I see Gramma coming, and freeze in my tracks. She doesn't see me and keeps walking. I turn back toward the school to avoid her. She spots me from a distance and we stare each other down—she realizes that I'm not letting her get any closer. We're two gunfighters in a standoff on Pond Street, Gramma versus Boy Kindergarten. Finally she retreats back home, all four-foot-two of her. I nonchalantly arrive a few minutes later and act like I don't know what's wrong.

Lugi, why you a no let me walk with you? You bad a boy!

I'm a big boy, Gramma, I want to walk alone.

You bad a boy, Lugi. How you a know that a man not gonna get you? I know a little boy and he no walk with his Gramma and a man come and a get him.

Gramma knows enough little boys to fit any circumstance. She once knew a boy who didn't stop playing with his belly button and his ass fell off.

My rebellion against Gramma began earlier that summer, at the 1965 World's Fair in New York City. The whole family took the train to New York, including Aunt Ro, Gramma, and Grampa. In the bustle of the crowd, Gramma's constant nagging left me no alternative but to wander off alone. I'm jubilant to get away from Gramma—*that'll fix her*—until I lose sight of my group

You bad a boy, Lugi.

and panic. A big policeman saves me, and carries the terrified boy back to his parents, tears streaming down his face. Instead of looking relieved that I'm safe and sound, Dad shows displeasure with me for scaring everybody. Why isn't he mad at Gramma for starting all the trouble?

Gramma says, *You bad a boy, Lugi.*

And I'm right back where I started.

••••

Dad leaves for work early in the mornings—especially if the construction site is far away. He keeps his construction hat in the car and wears jeans, work boots, and a tee-shirt. When he was selling insurance, he had to dress up every day—but he likes this better. Mom serves the family meal at six, giving Dad enough time to get home and preside over dinner. He often makes us laugh, coming in through the back door and yelling out, *Yoo-hoo, anybody home?* But the laughter quickly fades between the lovebirds. Mom calls to him.

Leo, get cleaned up, supper's almost ready!

Cripes, Annie, I just walked in the door. Don't you think I know that?

Listen to you, Mouth Almighty.

If I didn't work, there wouldn't be any supper.

Oh shut up.

Geeez!

Dad changes his clothes in the cellar and washes himself in the deep sink next to the washing machine. He comes upstairs and says, *Get me a beer, Louis.* He's the only one in the family who calls me Louis. Mom and Dad briefly kiss and embrace. I wait for them to finish so

I can give Dad his beer and get back to playing. I'm confused because the families that I see on TV don't talk like that to each other before showing affection.

I hand a cold beer to Dad and he sits in his favorite chair, faded red with a matching footstool. It's Dad's chair, no mistake, with his impression worn deep into the padding from daily use. We're not allowed to sit there if Dad's home, and he makes a sweeping motion with his hand to signal our instant departure from his chair, no words required. It's dangerous to contradict him about his chair, and never successful. Dad reads the headlines in the newspaper and looks content. He catches his second wind and goes into the kitchen to pepper Mom with a flurry of questions about her cooking.

Got enough salt in it? How long didja cook it? Where'd you buy this? How much did that cost? That's expensive—good thing I'm working or we wouldn't have any supper. That's all I'm good for—paying the bills!

Mom says, *Oh shut up, would you? You won't be happy unless we all choke. You give me agita.*

I want them to hug and kiss and make the house happy again.

Dad calls us for dinner. If we don't respond immediately we're sent to our rooms until he decides to call us again. We need to demonstrate that we know how to come when called *the first time.* He allows us to sit at the table, but gives us dirty looks while we take our places.

Mom says, *All right Leo, that's enough, let's say grace.*

In the name of the Father, the Son, and the Holy Spirit.

Bless us, O Lord, and these thy gifts, which we are about to receive from your bounty. Through Christ our Lord. Amen.

In the name of the Father, the Son, and the Holy Spirit.

I'm sitting next to Mom and she says, *Lugi, you didn't fold your hands right. Do you still think you don't need to go to Assumption?*

I look silently into my plate.

Dad says, *Answer your Mother, Louis. Show me how you fold your hands and ask God to forgive you.*

I'm not hungry anymore, and look forward to hearing that I'm excused.

· · ·

We're all afraid of Dad, but it's fun to try to pull one over on him while he's asleep in bed. In the wee hours of the morning Leo whispers for me to be quiet and we'll go downstairs and fix him good. I've just woken up, but tell him okay and get out of bed. I follow Leo past Terry's room. The wooden stairs creak on the way down and he scowls at me with a finger on his lips, looking much his father's son. We make the descent, and Leo stealthily peeks into our parents' room and tiptoes his way to Mom's side of the bed. He slowly opens the small drawer in the headboard and selects an ugly pink hairnet. Somehow he achieves the extraction without making a sound. I hold my breath, watching while he makes his way to his victim, hairnet in hand. The room remains quiet except for breathing sounds when he fastens the hairnet to Dad's skull. Like a junior Picasso, he pauses for a moment to admire his work before making a silent escape. We slip away into the living room, trying hard to muffle our laughter.

Dad awakens a little while later, and we listen intently to his footsteps headed into the bathroom. We hear the noise of his streaming emission, closely followed by the toilet flushing and water running in the sink. After Dad sees himself in the bathroom mirror he yells out *HEYYY!* Terry and Mom startle awake, and Leo and I go into hiding behind the furniture, busting a gut trying not to laugh.

• • •

CHAPTER TWO

THE SCIENCE CLUB

We love the fall weather and play outside every chance we get. Our cramped car ride to school has made us close friends with the Vinciguerras, and along with Nicky right next door, a small gang of boys begins to form. I want the Gacioch boys to join us. I see Timmy standing on his front lawn across the street and walk over to talk to him. His mother sees us and calls Timmy inside on some pretense. His face is soon visible in the front window, looking out. I feel sorry for him. I ask Mom if she thinks Timmy will ever cross the street.

I don't know, Lugi, maybe someday when he's allowed to leave their front yard.

I know Mom, but Timmy is my age and I think he wants to play.

How do you know he's your age?

Bobby told me.

How does he know?

I don't know, but he told me that Timmy's mother said he can't play with us.

Mom ponders this for a moment, her pride aroused.

I don't know what to tell you, Lugi, but they're not Italian. Where do those Gaciochs come from, anyway? Who does she think she is, not letting her boys play with you? They're not too good for you—you're too good for them! I think you're better off, Lugi.

But Mom, I don't even know them—and Timmy seems like he's nice.

Oh go out and play, I'm busy!

Mom's funny. She gets mad because Mrs. Gacioch won't let her boys play with us, and then she tells me that I can't play in Nicky's yard anymore.

Why can't I play in Nicky's yard, Mom? He's allowed to play with us, and he's here all the time.

Because you're always stepping in dog poop and bringing it in my house. Now go out and play before I make you stay in.

The Kenwick boys gather in our backyard, and we start the Science Club. I want to call it the Science Fair, but Leo says no. Nicky becomes the leader because he's the oldest, plus he owns a junior scientist kit. He performs experiments with all kinds of different chemicals in little test tubes, and makes up names for formulas that never do anything but make different colors. He keeps a list of his formulas anyway.

Why did you call that one puke, Nicky?

Cause that's what it looks like. Want me to mix you up a batch? I'll show ya.

No, that's okay, maybe some other time.

Nicky wants to locate the club headquarters at his house, but I tell him we can't because my Mom said I'm always stepping in poop. Bobby backs me up.

Yeah, Nicky—my Mom said I can't come home with dog poop either. Let's have it at Lugi's house—they don't have a dog.

Our backyard garage finally finds its true purpose: it becomes headquarters for the Science Club. It takes at least two of us to open the garage door, but only one to close it. It's fun! You get a running start from the back of the garage and jump up to grab one of the handles to get it moving. Then you put your foot on the bottom handle and hang on for the ride.

Our garage contains an old wooden cabinet about the size of a college dorm room fridge. Most of its red paint is peeled away. The hinges need repair and the cabinet door drags against the concrete floor whenever it's opened or closed. Still, it's perfect for us to store club materials like empty jars... for caterpillars, cocoons, bees, and anything else we can catch.

•••

It's my fifth birthday in October, and Mrs. Gruender interrupts the class for a special announcement. I'm surprised to see Mom and this other lady standing behind her holding boxes of cupcakes. I start to feel embarrassed when my teacher speaks.

Boys and girls, if it's your birthday today, I want you to raise your hand!

I shoot my hand up and the class starts to giggle. A few kids start going *Oooh-Oooh!* I don't know what they're Oooh-Ooohing for, and look around the room. There's a girl with her hand up, too. I want to tell her it's *my* birthday, put your hand down. More kids join the chorus of *Oooh-Oooh!* and she starts to turn red.

Mrs. Gruender says, *Louis and Marybeth, come up to the front of the class and we'll sing Happy Birthday to you both.*

I'm looking at Mom, confused. It's *my* birthday, what's *she* got to do with it?

Louis and Marybeth both have the same birthday, class! What do you think of that?

Now the entire Kindergarten class goes *Oooh-Oooh!* And finally, I get it. The two moms smile and I look at the red-faced, curly-haired girl hiding behind her mother. The class begins to sing, and I observe that she's a pretty little thing. Waves of puppy love flood over me, and my heart starts to go *Oooh-Oooh!*

After the song ends, I summon the courage to talk to her. She tells me to go play with the boys.

• • •

I know that the attic adjoining our upstairs hallway is haunted. I'm scared of what's inside. The attic is six feet deep, running the length of the hallway, with a short, narrow door halfway down the hall from the stairs. You have to bend over to enter, and the ceiling follows a steep roof line. Pointy roof nails protrude from above, making it look like a torture chamber. One bare light bulb with a pull string hangs just far enough from the door for me to imagine being grabbed by a ghoul, right before I can yank it on.

Leo and Terry appeal to Mom that their age entitles them to stay up later than me, and they often get their wish. I counter with a stalling tactic. If that fails, I wait at the top of the stairs for them. Better to wait and face ridicule than risk an encounter with a fiend from hell who lives in the attic.

Mom says, *Okay, kids, it's time for bed.*

I'm older than Lugi, Leo protests. *Make him go first.*

Terry echoes, *Yeah, Mom, make him go first.*

I glare dirty looks at them, but Mom caves in.

Lugi, you have to go to bed first.

But Mom...

But nothing, Lugi, get going!

I'm ready with a stalling tactic.

Okay Mom, I just have to go to the bathroom first.

Unfortunately for me, I'm also afraid of the shadowy hallway that flanks the bathroom door, so I jump from the dining room into the bathroom to limit my exposure. Everyone knows this, and they all laugh, but I don't care because at least I'm still alive. After a lengthy delay I hear Mom calling me.

I don't hear the toilet flushing, Lugi.

I yell, *Okay, Mom,* and flush the toilet, giving away my charade.

A few minutes later she says, *What are you doing in there now, Lugi?*

Just cleaning up, Mom!

I don't hear the water running!

I say, *Okay, Mom,* and turn on the water.

A few more minutes go by and she asks me again what I'm doing.

I put a toothbrush in my mouth and try to sound like I'm brushing my teeth.

The delay continues, Dad utters a loud threat and I'm out the bathroom door.

I jump from the bathroom to the foot of the stairs in the dining room, and everyone laughs again. It takes a long time to ascend the stairs, and there's so many of them. First step... second step... third step....

What's taking so long?

Nothing, Mom, I'm just tired.

Good, then get in bed and go to sleep.

Okay, Mom, can you tuck me in?

I'll be up later.

That's okay, Mom, I don't mind waiting for you.

No. Get going!

Okay, Mom. Fourth step... fifth step... sixth step...

I said get going!

I reach the top landing and freeze upon seeing the attic door halfway down the hall to my bedroom.

A minute goes by and Mom's patience is wearing thin.

I know you're still up there, Lugi. Get going! Nothing is going to get you—just turn on the hallway light!

Mom doesn't know that the hallway light won't stop the attic door from opening by itself, or me from getting dragged inside, never to be seen again. But I do.

I hear Leo and Terry laughing, so I take a few loud steps in place and silently remain at the landing. I tremble, glancing at the attic door to make sure it's still closed and I'm not being pursued. Leo can't control himself and sneaks over to the stairs.

He's still up there, Mom! I can see him!

Good, I'm glad to hear it. And now you can go to bed, too!

But, Mom...!

*But nothing, Leo, **get going!***

He starts grumbling that I'm going to get it. His face looks scarier than whatever lives in the attic. I sprint down the hallway past the attic door. In our room I accept the pain from his punches. It's the lesser of two evils... but it still hurts.

•••

Halloween arrives a week after my birthday. It's for Science Club members only, no girls allowed. Our sisters wear typical girly stuff like princess or ballerina costumes. We go trick-or-treating without 'em.

But mine glows in the dark.

The Science Club assembles. Leo is the Thing from the Fantastic Four, I'm Frankenstein, and we're met by Dracula, the Wolfman, a ghost, and an astronaut. Plastic masks fasten to our heads with a rubber band, and flimsy costumes complete the garb. Mom wants me to wear a jacket, but it hides my costume, so I appease her with an extra sweatshirt and I'm out the front door. Mom yells her final instructions.

Don't stay out too late! And make sure you stay on Kenwick!

The fun begins! We use pillowcases to carry our haul of full-size candy bars. The sacks soon get heavy. We don't get far before the mask makes my face perspire and creates little pools of sweat inside the contours of the plastic. The fresh air feels good whenever I take the mask off to shake the sweat out of it.

We just went to a house that gave us giant Nestle's Crunch bars, and David gets greedy.

He says, *Let's switch masks and go back—they won't know it's us.*

So we make the switch and ring the doorbell. The homeowners laugh upon seeing the same masks again at different heights that don't match the costumes, but we get more Crunch bars. The ruse mostly works at other houses. Whenever we're turned away, I don't understand how they know it's us again.

It's thrilling to be out alone at night with my friends! I wish that Halloween came more than once a year. After going up one side of Kenwick Drive and back down the other we return home with full pillowcases that aren't empty until Thanksgiving, or ignored after all the good stuff is gone—whichever comes first.

•••

Thanksgiving arrives and Mom's busy cooking up a storm. She boils the turkey giblets in a pot, and we argue over who gets to eat the neck. Dad tells us we're lucky for all of this food. When he grew up, they all fought over who got to eat the turkey heart, that's how poor they were. Mom doesn't want to hear it.

Oh, here we go again, Leo. I'll ask the butcher to fix me a bag of turkey hearts and you can eat them all— maybe then you'll get over it.

Mom is skilled in sarcasm. She throws in a closing shot.

Kids, don't eat the turkey heart, that's for your father. He grew up poor, did you know that?

Dad gives her a look and sighs a long *Geeez*. Then he breaks out in a song that nobody ever heard, sung to the tune of the children's song, *Frere Jacques*.

Next Thanksgiving,
Next Thanksgiving,
Don't eat bread,
Don't eat bread,
Shove it up the turkey,
Shove it up the turkey,
Eat the bird,
Eat the bird.

Geeez, we never ate like this when I was a kid.

Gramma, Grampa, and Aunt Ro come over for Thanksgiving dinner and for once we get to eat in the dining room. Gramma brings a big pot of her chicken soup with greens and little meatballs. She ladles out bowls for everyone.

How come you no put any cheese on it, it's a better that way.

Okay, Gramma, pass me the cheese.

You good a boy, Lugi. She likes me when I eat.

I want to ask her if she knows a little boy that didn't put sprinkle cheese on his chicken soup and find out what happened to him, but I'm too hungry to bother.

After the soup is cleared away, Gramma serves a big pan of homemade manicotti stuffed with ricotta cheese and covered in fresh tomato sauce.

But Gramma, it's Thanksgiving—we want turkey!

You eat this first. It's good a fo' you.

Do I have to?

You bad a boy, Lugi. You no mind you Gramma.

Okay, Gramma, pass me the cheese.

You good a boy, Lugi!

The way to Gramma's heart is through my stomach.

The golden brown turkey finally hits the table. I hear stomachs growling. After the soup and manicotti there's only room in my stomach for part of a wing and I can't finish the mashed potatoes and stuffing on my plate. Since Dad grew up poor he only allows clean plates.

Louis, finish everything on your plate.

But Dad, I'm full, I say in a whiny voice.

You have to eat everything on your plate, Louis. Did you eat everything?

Everything but a little mashed potatoes and the stuffing on my plate, Dad.

No, I meant did you have some of everything on the table?

He knows that I didn't. The torment continues.

Did you have any cranberry sauce?

No Dad, I don't like it.

Did you try it?

No Dad, I don't like it.

How do you know you don't like it if you don't try it?

He spoons some on my plate and tells me to eat it. I frown and manage to force the cranberry sauce down my throat with many sips of ginger ale. Then Dad realizes a major oversight.

Did you have any sweet potatoes?

I hate sweet potatoes more than cranberry sauce and everything else, except maybe squash.

No, Dad, I wanted to make sure that there was some for everybody else.

Don't you get smart with me mister, Dad snarls, and plops a big chunk of nauseating orange sweet potatoes on my plate.

The putrid sight recalls to mind one of Nicky's science formulas—the one called puke. Then a strange thing happens. Gramma leans over and starts nibbling away at my sweet potatoes! I'm glad to let her. Dad notices Gramma's passive aggressive act, everybody else notices Dad noticing Gramma, and suddenly nobody is talking anymore. After a few tense minutes of Gramma's nibbling, the silence gets to Mom and she cracks.

Oh, for God's sake, Leo, leave him alone! He ate enough! And please spare me another story of how poor you were as a child! You'll give us all agita.

Dad gives her a long-suffering look and sighs another long *Geeez.*

Gramma keeps nibbling away at the remains on my plate, and soon it's all gone.

I love Gramma, and vow to always sit next to her whenever I can. The dinner table is cleared. Once nobody's looking, I throw out most of the leftover sweet potatoes with great delight. Soon I'm hungry again for chocolate pie with fresh whipped cream!

• • •

I still believe in Santa Claus. I'm worried he won't know that we moved. Mom tells me to write him a letter, so I look for a pen and paper. Leo looks relieved, but Terry shakes her head with a smirk. Mom catches her.

Don't you go spoiling it for them, Terry!

But Mom, there's...

But nothing, Terry.

Spoiling what, Mom? I ask.

Never mind, just get the paper!

Dear Santa,

I don't live upstairs from Gramma anymore. We moved to Kenwick Drive next to where Bobby lives. Leo went pee on the side of the house and the lady across the street yelled at him but he said he was sorry. I want a Tonka truck for Christmas and we have a real fireplace now so be careful if Dad makes a fire. Terry said I called her a name but I didn't and she beat me up. I was a good boy this year and I'll be nice to Gramma. I told Mom not to burn the cookies.

Love, Lugi

Now it's time to decorate the house. We all go upstairs to drag boxes of Christmas stuff from the attic. I'm not afraid of the attic if there's other people around, but I won't go in there alone. Terry notices this and calls me a big baby. After we bring all the boxes downstairs, Mom clears the fireplace mantel to make room for the Nativity scene. It's an Italian household, so there's lots of knick-knacks on the mantel. She moves them to the already crowded bookshelves on both sides of the fireplace. There's so many of them that we call it Knick-Knack Mountain. I picture Mom making a small fortune in a yard sale.

Want a candy dish? Sure, I got seven of 'em.

How about an ashtray? I got ten, pick out a nice one!

Need a porcelain statue? There's all kinds of people, angels—animals, too. Which one do ya want? That little shoemaker guy is kinda cute, don'tcha think? Hmmm... Maybe I won't sell that one...

Mom likes her Nativity scene more than the Christmas tree. It's got a wooden stable and little statues of the Holy Family, various animals, a couple of angels, shepherds and wise men making their approach. She takes her time to get it right, and doesn't want us to bother her while she's working.

Mom, can we have lunch now? I'm hungry.

No—you wait till I'm done.

Mom, Terry's making a face at me.

Tell her to stop.

Mom, Lugi farted.

Good, I hope it stinks!

Mom's Nativity scene happens at the North Pole. There's lots of snow and I look for Rudolph and Santa on the stable roof. She wads up newspaper to make hills and covers everything with rolls of cotton to make it winter outside. My illustrated Children's Bible missed the part of the story where Joseph hangs outdoor lights on the stable eaves—the first miracle of Christmas. Mom attaches a cotton ball of snow to the last light. It hangs precariously above the manger and the baby's head. It all looks nice to Mom, though. She steps back to admire her work.

The Blizzard of Bethlehem

Leo, Jr. says, *Mom, I don't think it snows in the desert.*

Shut up—I like it!

Terry says, *But Mom, the shepherds are barefoot!*

Who asked you?

I chime in, *Mom, where does Mary plug in the lights?*

I see the look on her face and don't wait for an answer.

The once-a-year airing of Rudolph the Red Nosed Reindeer comes on TV tonight, and we're excited to watch it. Dad makes popcorn on the stove and Mom gives us big glasses of Kool Aid to wash it down. I turn on our console television and feel rich sitting on the floor in a front row seat right by the logs crackling in our fireplace.

Somebody says *Change the channel, Lugi, it's on the wrong station!*

I turn the dial to one of the other two channels that work. Channel 24, the PBS station, comes in lousy so it doesn't count. Everybody likes the Rudolph cartoon and the TV commercials with the elves sledding downhill on Norelco shavers. Rudolph's reindeer girlfriend Clarice makes me dream of Marybeth... maybe someday she'll talk to me. And that song she sings... about *There's always tomorrow...*

Santa finds our house on Christmas Eve all right. We tear through the presents under the tree early on Christmas morning. There's more proof that Santa exists, too. The cookies are gone, and Mom points to a mark behind the grate in the fireplace.

Lugi, do you see that black mark at the back of the fireplace? That's where Santa burned his ass—ha ha ha.

• • •

It's the blizzard of 1966. School's cancelled, and we feel like going outside to play in the snow.

Mom, we want to make a snow cave like where the Abominable Snowman lives.

Okay, but you have to get bundled up first so that you don't freeze.

It's taking forever for me to get bundled up. I can't keep up with Leo and Terry.

I can't put on another sweatshirt, Mom, it won't fit.

You do what I say or you're not going out!

I want to go out so I don't argue. Leo already put the plastic bags over his shoes, and plunked his feet into wobbly rubber boots that buckle in the front.

I'm done, Mom, he says.

All right—go and help your Dad shovel.

Okay, Mom, and he's out the front door.

I start to panic but take consolation from Terry's whining for Mom to help her find her snow pants. During their search I finish bundling up.

Our driveway adjoins the Savastanos', leaving but one side for Dad to throw the snow. He keeps shoveling, and soon it starts to look like a small mountain at the end by the street. I look up at the snowbank from the driveway, pondering how to reach the summit, let alone dig out a cave.

I'll show ya how to get up there, Leo says.

He takes a running start and launches himself onto the mountain. I watch him kick and claw his way upward and soon he's standing at the top smiling down at me.

C'mon up, he beckons from the summit.

I try to use his method, but bounce off the snow pile and land back in the driveway. Leo laughs at my repeated failures and says he's king of the mountain. I try to make snowballs to throw at him but it's not good packing snow. He taunts me.

Terry finds her snow pants. I'm frustrated at how easily she joins Leo at the peak. They're both making fun of me now, and my frustration turns into rage. Dad notices my distress and heaves me onto the mountain, high enough for me to climb the rest of the way. I start kicking and clawing like Leo did and get to the top. I'm not mad anymore, but I try to push Terry down when she's not looking. She turns to bare her teeth, and soon I'm halfway back down to the driveway. I change strategies and say *Let's dig a cave for the snowman!* Terry reminds me of the Abominable. If we dig a cave for her, maybe she'll move in.

Terry says, *I'm cold!*

Leo says, *Me, too, let's go back inside.*

I cast a confused look and say, *Are you kidding?*

We descend the mountain and trudge our way through the snow, up the front steps, and back into the house. Mom is not happy to see us.

You're back already? Next time don't bother me unless you stay out longer. I should make you go back outside!

Sometimes we spend more time getting bundled and unbundled than playing outside in the snow.

...

CHAPTER THREE

PAULY THE POOPER

Assumption Catholic provides its students with a sound education, along with a healthy fear of God, nuns, and priests—but especially nuns. The nuns at Assumption come from the Franciscan Order, clothed all in black beneath a dark veil except for the head, neck, and face framed in white, right up to the chin. All skin remains covered except for the face and hands, and not much arm past the wrist. It looks uncomfortable, and I don't know how they endure the many layers of dark clothing on warm days. The restrictive attire likely contributes to their bad moods. Gramma sometimes calls them Black Devils.

The Kindergarten school year draws to a close and feelings of apprehension fill my mind. I want Mrs. Gruender again. I don't think that I'll like the nuns so much. For a brief moment I imagine seeing the outline of a nun in our attic, crouched over the box of Halloween masks.

Sr. Mary Walter teaches Leo's first grade class. Both of my siblings say she's mean, alluding to her long, wooden pointer-whipping stick, and the occasional rap of a small head against the blackboard. Both administered in consequence of giving the wrong answer. Six-year-olds need encouragement, and she literally pounds knowledge into their heads if required—she loves her kids that much.

Leo recently experienced this peculiar display of affection. His tale made me shiver.

She wrote arithmetic problems on the chalkboard and made a few of us solve them right in front of the whole class.

Were you nervous to stand in front of the class?

Yes, but you do whatever she tells you to. Don't ask stupid questions!

What happened next?

I wrote my answer on the board and waited for her while she corrected the other kids' answers first. She got right up close to Joyce, put the pointer on the blackboard, and kept asking her, Are you sure, are you sure? Joyce changed her answer and got it right the second time. Then the same thing happens with the other kids— they fix the answers to get it right. When it's finally my turn she puts the pointer on the board and says, Are you sure, are you sure? And I wasn't sure, so I erase the right answer and make it wrong.

What did she do?

She got really mad and corrected the answer with chalk. I'm watching the pointer expecting to get hit but instead she grabs my ear and bashes my head into the blackboard. She said, This will help you to remember!

I don't want to feel the whipping stick or get my head bashed into the blackboard, so I ask Mom if I can change schools.

Mom, I want to go to Lyncourt School next year so I won't have Sr. Mary Walter. I'll be good, Mom. Can I go there instead?

No, you're going to Assumption. Leo and Terry both survived. Don't be a big baby!

But, Mom...

But nothing, Lugi. Just pray for her every night, and God will make her be nice to you.

That night I started.

Dear God, please make Sr. Mary Walter be nice to me and please make her not hit me with the pointer and please make her not rap my head against the blackboard.

God hears my prayers. Soon Mom tells me that Sr. Liam is taking over the first grade in the fall. She's new to the convent and to teaching at Assumption. Mom says that before Sr. Liam became a nun she worked with Aunt Ro at the telephone company, and she's nice.

Just give her a chance, Lugi. You'll see.

At five years old I start to believe in miracles and divine intervention. Thank you, God!

•••

Kindergarten ends, and the good weather and no school means a lot of kids playing in our backyard. Mrs. Wilson lives directly behind us with a short, rickety wooden fence demarcating the property line between our two backyards. She looks at least a hundred years old but maintains a liking for strong drink. For reasons unknown, the activities of the Science Club get her riled up. She calls over the fence.

Youse kids! Hey, youse kids!

Yes, whaddya want?

Hey! Don't you talk to me that way!

Well, you called us, so whaddya want?

Mrs. Wilson makes her way to the fence in in a long, irregular arc, blinking hard. At close range we smell the unmistakable fragrance of booze. All of our Dads share Mrs. Wilson's fondness for spirits, so we're familiar with the aroma in addition to its other side effects. I'm confused because I assume her condition can only be achieved by men at clambakes, generally ending with orange blobs of littleneck clams from Hinerwadel's on the rug and Dad asleep on the floor.

She shakes a fist at us and struggles to maintain focus.

Youse kids! You just keep it down with all that racket. Some people gotta work!

Several members of the club answer her at once, adding to her confusion.

Working? Who's working? It's Saturday!

You're not working—you're drinking!

Since when is drinking working?

Did you just get home from a clambake, old lady? Ha!

Dad notices the commotion and walks to the back fence to see what's going on.

Dad, she's drunk and she said for us to keep it down because some people gotta work. Tell her it's Saturday, Dad, she don't believe us.

A clambake veteran with high honors, Dad quickly assesses her condition, smiles, and politely asks, *Is there a problem here?*

Not the least bit intimidated, Mrs. Wilson sizes him up, still squinting.

Oh, look at you! Think you're a big man, don't you?

Once more Dad smiles and repeats, *Is there a problem here?*

Mrs. Wilson believes that Dad fathered all of the kids she sees before her, and confronts him.

There's a problem, all right. You oughtta learn to keep that thing in your pants—all you're good for is makin' babies!

Dad laughs and retreats to the house. Along the way he shakes his head and sighs, *Geeez.*

• • •

Little Pauly Vinciguerra smiles and wanders. Now he's getting potty trained and wears big boy pants. He surprises neighbors not expecting to find him in their yards, and he's a man of few words.

What are you doing, Pauly?

Nothin'.

Does your mother know where you are?

No.

Pauly and his older brothers Bobby and David make themselves at home at our house and often let themselves in without ringing the doorbell. Leo and I don't care because we're the same way at their house. You only ring the doorbell if you want somebody to come out, otherwise you just walk in and start playing.

Dad and the Vinciguerra boys

We like to play with toy trucks underneath the pine tree in our backyard—we call it the Christmas tree. It's fun to excavate tunnels underneath the tree roots and drive our vehicles through them. I'm going back to the tree with a dump truck loaded with matchbox cars, and encounter Pauly heading in the opposite direction. He doesn't say anything, but smiles and waves at me. I'm driving cars into the tunnels and the wheel of my dump tuck barely misses a couple of little brown turds.

I imagine the turds came from one of the neighborhood dogs, so I grab a shovel from the garage in our backyard. I glance around to make sure that nobody's watching and heave the turds into Mrs. Wilson's yard. No harm done, it's only Mrs. Wilson's slippers at risk. I forget all about it.

Once again I find turds after seeing Pauly walking away. I share my suspicions.

Mom, I really think Little Pauly goes poop under the Christmas tree.

How do you know, Lugi?

*I keep finding little turds, Mom, and it's always af-
ter he's been back there alone.*

Well, if you catch him you just let me know, okay?

Okay, Mom—I'll catch him all right!

Bobby & Pauly Vinciguerra

I run a police stakeout of our backyard, anxious to
catch Pauly committing the crime of defecation under
the Christmas tree. As honey draws flies, the Christmas
tree beckons to Pauly and it's not long before he's appre-
hended. I spy him in a squatting position and it looks
like he's pushing hard. I sound the alarm.

**Mom! Pauly's going poop under the Christmas
tree again!**

Mom jumps into action and hollers at Pauly from the kitchen window.

Hey! You go home and poop in your own yard!

Mom startles Pauly but he quickly recovers, pulls up his pants, and keeps smiling all the way home. I admire Pauly for his cool demeanor—I'd turn three shades of red and melt into the ground if I ever got caught going poop under somebody's Christmas tree. I consider the turd mystery solved, but Leo says that sometimes Bobby plays under the Christmas tree alone, and then we find bigger turds. Bobby's a fast learner, though. Hearing of Pauly's capture, he no longer plays alone under the Christmas tree. Leo never catches Bobby with his pants down, and Mrs. Wilson never steps in the poop that I throw over her fence. It's not right that people get away with shit like this.

•••

Dad likes to drink beer every time he cooks on the charcoal grill, usually a cold Genesee. *Go get me a beer, Louis,* he says. I'm the official beer getter. He likes to smoke stinky cigars, too, and I'm often dispatched for stogies and matches.

He piles up the charcoal into a little pyramid, and douses it with lighter fluid before taking a big gulp of beer.

When ya gonna light it, Dad?

The lighter fluid needs to soak in, Louis.

He takes another swig.

I love to watch the big flames erupt, and ask permission to light it.

No, Louis, you'll get burned.

Aw, c'mon Dad, let me light it—I'll be careful!

I said no.

And his frown ends the discussion.

We stand there watching the flames. Dad drinks more beer. When the fire burns low, he says, *Go get me a fanning board, Louis.* Dad's fanning boards come from the old ceiling tiles strewn about the floor of the backyard garage. The Science Club makes use of ceiling tiles, too—many flying or crawling insects end their lives nailed to one. I retrieve a board for Dad, and he fans the charcoal with a great force, creating millions of orange sparks. The lighter fluid burns away and the charcoal catches fire from Dad's exertions.

Get me a beer, Louis.

I go to retrieve another cold Genny. Upon arriving back outside I'm surprised to find Little Pauly, Bobby, David, Nicky, and Leo playing in our backyard. I give Dad his beer and watch him fan the fire again for a while before joining in with the others.

Suddenly I see that Pauly's face, lips and hands have taken on the same color as the charcoal and it's not hard to make the connection. Confronted with the evidence, Pauly smiles. His black teeth incriminate him further. Dad looks at Pauly and says, *Geeez.*

I ask him, *Pauly, you eating charcoal?*

No.

You're gonna get sick, Pauly, go rinse your mouth! What's wrong with you?

Nothin'.

A few days later Pauly's face once again turns black after he's been playing near the bag of charcoal in our backyard garage.

Mom! Pauly's eating charcoal again!

Mom jumps into action and hollers at Pauly from the kitchen window.

Hey! You go home and eat your own charcoal!

Pauly startles but quickly recovers. He calmly wipes the charcoal off his face on the back of his shirt sleeve and keeps smiling, not a care in the world.

•••

Insects captured by the Science Club routinely face a sentence of death by impalement to a ceiling tile, and they live the scant remaining hours of their lives as prisoners on death row. The insect Green Mile consists of various glass jars stored in the red wooden cabinet, and we place new arrivals in jars with air holes in the lids until the speedy appeals process concludes. No rights of appeal exist for large insects, types never impaled, or ones with unique colors. The fates of others are determined mostly by the availability of ceiling tiles. After confirmation of their death sentence, they're transferred to jars with solid lids because we want them to pass out. This way they won't wiggle their way to escape during impalement, and they're less likely to bite or sting the executioner.

It's a safety thing, and if they're unconscious we figure it limits our club's exposure to lawsuits from prisoner and animal rights groups alike.

The club decides to create a bug display at headquarters. Everyone gets involved. Our president, Nicky, assigns various tasks like sweeping the floor, wiping away cobwebs, stacking ceiling tiles, and various other custodial duties. He says that because he's the president he gets to pick the location of the bug tiles in the garage, though it's obvious that Leo's unhappy with his selections.

Overall it looks pretty nice, unusually clean and organized, and I begin to wonder if this is actually my garage. The daydream is interrupted by the sound of Nicky's Dad calling for him. Nicky answers, *Okay Dad,* but doesn't go. The calls and replies repeat several times more, with Nicky blissfully ignorant of the imminent danger. Suddenly, Mr. Savastano bursts onto the scene with Nicky's play guitar firmly grasped in his right hand, way up high on the neck. With his free hand he grabs Nicky by the arm, spins him around, and blasts Nicky's ass with the body of the guitar, sending splinters flying everywhere. Nicky screams loud enough to wake the dead while being admonished by his Dad.

This will teach you to come when I call you, Nicky!

Then he gives his ass another blast with the remnants of Nicky's career in music. Nicky doesn't stop screaming, but it fades once Mr. Savastano gets him inside the house and the garage door closes.

No longer impeded by presidential power, Leo immediately rearranges every bug tile— demonstrating early symptoms of obsessive compulsive disorder. We don't know the clinical term for it—in our simple minds he's just weird. The guys whisper their concerns while Leo busily rearranges everything in the garage with a faraway look in his eyes.

Lugi, what's wrong with Leo?

I don't know.

Yeah, Lugi, why's he got to move everything around?

I don't know.

Is he like this all the time, Lugi?

Yes.

How can you stand it?

You should try sharing a room with him.

Then I blurt out, **Hey Leo, everybody thinks you're weird!**

Leo snaps out of his daze and upon hearing our diagnosis, punches me hard. I learn that despite good intentions it's impossible to help some people, especially relatives. Nobody in the club comes to my aid. I perceive there's a lot more to learn.

The club's anxious for other people to see the results of our hard work. Everybody runs home with invitations to see the bug museum, which stands empty for days. Some of the smaller bugs start to fall off the nails. We decide to take the show on the road so at least our Moms can see, and maybe ring a few doorbells along the way. The neighbors will love this—who wouldn't?

The Moms aren't happy to see dead bugs in their kitchens, impaled or not, but they force a smile. Some express remorse for the departed and others say *That's nice,* but all them quickly direct us back outside. The neighbors gawk and don't know what to say to the smiling, upturned faces they see behind the ceiling tiles full of impaled insects.

Isn't this cool?

There's still a bunch of unused tiles in the garage, and we need a decision from our club president about what to do with them. I go to find Nicky but stop as he comes running into our backyard, all excited.

Hey guys! My cat Tinker just had a big litter of kittens!

We're all anxious to see the kittens but Nicky says we can't. His Dad told him to leave Tinker and her kittens alone, and he'll get in big trouble if he bothers them. We're resigned to stay away until Mr. Savastano says so, but the delay provides Terry with time to contemplate ways to ask Mom for a cat. She already knows the answer, but I follow her inside to watch. Once safely on the opposite side of our dining room table from Mom she asks her.

So Mom, do you think we could ever have a cat?

No.

Well, how about a kitten, then?

No.

Mom, did you know the Savastanos' cat had kittens?

No.

Can I ask Mr. Savastano for one, Mom?

No.

I watch the spectacle unfold, observing Mom begin to circle the table while Terry steps around at the same pace to maintain her distance. I never witnessed Ring around the Rosie played like this. The game continues.

*So Mom, I **really** want a cat and I'll take care of it!*

No.

*Oh please, Mom, **please?***

No.

The pace quickens and Mom suddenly stops to put her foot down, as it were. Terry doesn't stop in time and finds herself standing too close to Mom. She takes a couple steps backward for safety.

*I **don't** want a cat, Terry, and I'm **not** going to change my mind! **End of discussion!***

Oh Please** Mom, I'll take care of it, **I promise!

*I said **The End!***

Terry inherited Mom's disposition and matches her emotion with defiance.

*We're the **only** ones who **can't** have a pet. You **never** get me anything... and you're **mean!***

Mom's chasing her at full speed now. Our good Syracuse China dishes start to rattle in the cabinet while Terry runs for her life just out of her reach. Around and around they go.

You just wait 'til I get my hands on you, Terry!

Terry keeps running and gasps in terror. It's frightening for a young, loving, innocent child like me to even watch.

Ahhhh!

Stop running Terry!

No!!

I said stop!

No! Ahhhh!!

Having prior experience with guilt by association I decide it's a good time for me to go and play with the boys. I reach the back door, no longer hearing running noises or china plates rattling. Only Terry's hysterics inform me of her capture. I've endured several beatings at her hands, but I still feel sorry for her. Well, sort of.

Eventually the kittens age to Mr. Savastano's satisfaction. We're happy to see them, but Tinker's not happy to see us. She doesn't like people reaching into her box full of blankets and kittens.

At the first sight of the kittens Terry's encounter with Mom fades to ancient history, and she engages Nicky in conversation.

So Nicky, are you giving away any kittens?

One of my cousins said she wants one, and Dad told me to ask the neighbors about the others.

Oh, really?

I see the wheels turning in her head, and provide a speedy course correction.

You're not getting a cat, Terry, remember what Mom said.

Terry gives me a look to scare the devil in hell. I make a mental note to not let her catch me alone. I observed that same exact look on Mom's face recently while she circled the dining room table at high speed. And I know how it ended, too, so I better stay clear until the kitten box empties, plus a few extra days to play it safe. She's threatened my life before, and this might be the final straw.

Tinker proves herself a good mother and zealously guards her brood until one sad and fateful day. A year younger than me, Suzie Savastano hears that the kittens need a bath and she wants to help. Unfortunately, she doesn't wait for adult supervision and gives the kittens a bath in liquid Clorox bleach. The ensuing tragedy quickly unfolds. Mr. Savastano tries to give the kittens Pepto Bismol from an eye dropper. The intervention sadly fails despite a valiant effort, and all of the kittens expire. Suzie becomes distraught, and we all feel sorry for her because she meant well and didn't know any better. She's crying hard and everybody feels her pain. Nicky and his Dad wrap the dead kittens in newspaper and bury them in their backyard. A gloom hangs over their house, and the whole neighborhood remains unusually quiet.

Weeks later, several members of the Science Club become desirous of adding skeletal remains to the museum in our backyard garage. We're young scientists, ignorant of how long it takes for a body to decompose, so we petition our president for an answer.

Hey Nicky, how long do ya think that it takes for a dead cat to turn into bones? The instructions in your chemistry set say anything about it?

Hey Nicky, when will ya let us dig 'em up? We need the bones for our club.

Yeah, Nicky, we'll keep the bones safe in the cabinet. We promise, and you're still the president of the club, too!

That's right Nicky. And we'll put 'em on the top shelf with all our best stuff.

Nicky refuses our requests, but it's obvious that he's as eager as the rest of us. We keep after him. It's not long before he relents, and he even provides the shovel for the grave robbery. As he leads us to the kittens' tomb, I'm watching for landmines in the Savastanos' backyard left by Nicky's dog Lassie. The Science Club cautiously approaches the burial site. I let them go ahead of me.

It's easier to avoid dog shit if somebody else steps in it first. And Lassie's infamous for wet ones.

Our apprehension grows with each spade of dirt. Several faces peer intently at the opening grave. The shovel reveals newspaper and everyone leans in closer. The next scoop produces an orange-brown mush and the neighborhood echoes with loud screams emitted by fleeing members of the Science Club.

Yeuch!

Nicky lingers to restore the sleep of the dead, while hosing off the shovel. Safely next door the Science Club whimpers, hosing off dog shit from our sneaker bottoms.

Yeuch!

• • •

CHAPTER FOUR

THE GERMANS ARE NICER THAN THE ITALIANS

We spend many summer days hanging out in the Vinciguerras' backyard. Everybody likes to play Beatles and PT 109. Playing Beatles means strumming tennis racket guitars, putting on Beatles records, and loudly singing along, complete with improvised head shakes and screams. Whenever more than four of us play it results in multiple Johns and Pauls, maybe a George or two—but never more than one Ringo. Nobody ever wants to be Ringo. Little Pauly often fills this role and he protests with emotion to no avail. David hands him a couple of tree sticks and tells him to shut up if he knows what's good for him. We turn the record player up high, and our loud, high-pitched *Ooohh's* from *She Loves You* makes the neighborhood dogs howl, compelling Mrs. Vinciguerra to restore peace and quiet.

Every summer the Vinciguerras erect a round, three-foot-deep aboveground pool in their backyard. We use it to play PT 109, in tribute to John F. Kennedy's adventures in World War II. We reenact the famous scene of the PT boat getting sunk, and pretend we're the crew swimming to dry land by doing underwater laps around the pool. Every kid on the street likes to swim, and sometimes there's not enough room in the pool for all the PT boat survivors. Inevitably, somebody gets kicked in the head by the drowning man in front of him and fights erupt amongst the crew. Mrs. Vinciguerra again brings quiet to the neighborhood by sending everyone home.

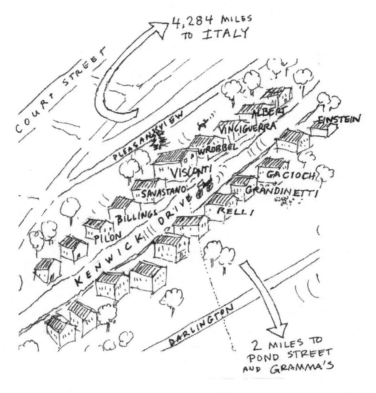

Mr. and Mrs. Albert emigrated from Germany, and they live next to the Vinciguerras on the side farther away from my house. They're nice people who live quietly and never complain about loud Beatles music, howling dogs, or swimming pool fights, and they let kids be kids. Mr. Albert takes great pride in the many flowers he cultivates, and can often be seen working in his yard. Sometimes he asks Terry to join him for a friendly tour of his latest blooms and she's always glad to oblige him.

We're playing at the Vinciguerras and something catches David's attention next door in the Alberts' backyard. He's compelled to get a closer look, and the only obstacle remaining is the Alberts' fence. It's your standard four-foot chain link fence. The kind that terminates in a row of equally spaced, intertwined pairs of fence wires projecting skyward at the top. The unforgiving kind, designed by sadists who don't like children, discouraging most kids from trying to climb over it. But we're not *most* kids—we know how to navigate this hazard. At least most of the time.

David's journey starts well, but ends short—just three-quarters of the way over. He slips at the top and screams as his arms, legs, face, and torso encounter the barbs on the way down. We groan in chorus, watching it all happen in what seems like slow motion. His trip ends on the Alberts' side of the fence, with David hanging there, tee-shirt and shorts caught in the merciless grip of the wire barbs at the top. It's a pitiful sight, amplified by shrieks of pain and terror. He hangs there on the fence in a weird position, twitching and flopping like a fish out of water—and like that fish, he's not going anywhere.

Mrs. V. hears the commotion and after what must be an eternity for the victim, she appears in the Alberts' yard to extract David from the fence. She makes quick work of it, motivated by sounds of crying and despair. She carries her boy back inside, his moans echoing up and down Kenwick Drive and around the block, too. Bobby and Little Pauly follow, quiet and subdued. The rest of us go home feeling a little queasy—at least I am.

David emerges later that day, again followed by Bobby and Pauly. He's covered from head to toe in an assortment of Band-Aids, gauze, and white medical tape. I envision an empty medicine cabinet in the Vinciguerras' house. David is bandaged like Boris Karloff in *The Mummy*. He looks kind of funny, but he's nice enough to pull back the wrappings for us to see the worst injuries. Some appear to be much deeper than others—it hurts just to look at them.

Two weeks go by before David again braves the fence, and he gets in big trouble after his Mom finds out.

• • •

Although most of my neighbors are Italian, the Alberts aren't the only first generation Germans on our block—and they're all older than my parents. Right across the street from the Alberts live the Einsteins. So on one side of Kenwick there's Albert and directly across there's Einstein, both right off the boat from the old country. With all this brilliance, it's hard for me to understand what they say in their heavy German accents—but there's no mistaking their smiles. Mr. Einstein likes to make chocolates. If he cooks a batch containing alcohol, he walks across the street to see if Mom would like to sample them, inviting her over in his deep German accent.

Mrs. Visconti, you've got to try zese! Come to my house, come to my house!

Mrs. Einstein sometimes waves from her front yard for my sister Terry to come visit her. She asks Terry to sit down in her kitchen and offers her fresh-baked molasses cookies. Terry tells me that Mrs. Einstein likes to talk to her, but she never says what they talk about. Mrs. Einstein keeps an impressive collection of Hummel figurines that's the envy of every girl on Kenwick Drive—but few enjoy the privilege of seeing them. Fresh cookies, pleasant conversation with Mrs. Einstein, and close proximity to the Hummel figurines make it a triple treat for my big sister.

The Wrobbels live in between us and the Vinciguerras. Like ours, their attached garage opens into the backyard and their cars remain parked in the driveway, day or night, rain or shine. The Wrobbel girls, Patty and Diane, are Leo and Terry's ages, but they're only friends with Terry because Leo and I don't play with girls. Neither one of them ever pays any attention to me unless I provoke them. I enjoy pestering the sisters, especially Diane, if it's a slow day and it looks like they're having a little too much fun playing with Terry. I figure that I'm entitled to impose on Terry whenever I've a mind to, her being a blood relative and all. The girls disagree, and Diane restrains me while Terry strikes and Patty watches. Then they take turns—but Patty just watches. She's a nice girl.

There are other older Wrobbels, too, but they're too old to play with anyone that I know. Their front yard becomes the neutral zone in our not infrequent rock wars with the Vinciguerras, and one Wrobbel or another always puts an end to our epic battles. They order an immediate end to hostilities and that clean-up commence, post-haste. The opposing armies share a common resentment for any Wrobbel who dares to ruin a good rock fight.

Across the street from the Savastanos live Mr. and Mrs. Relli. They're the same age as my parents, well, maybe a little older. Mr. Relli drives a shiny new Cadillac and he gives it many baths while his wife works on their landscaping. Their yard always looks pristine, with a variety of finely trimmed shrubbery that rivals the Alberts' up the street.

Mrs. Relli puts a lot of effort into her prize landscaping. She fiercely guards it from the marauding Science Club, especially when we're in search of bugs. Her fuse is short when it comes to her garden, and she chases us away.

Go home, you little WOPs!

She married an Italian, but must not be one or she wouldn't call us little WOPs. I want Mr. Relli to catch her using the W word, but he never does.

Right across the street from us and next door to the Rellis live the Grandinettis, another Irish clan. Terry Grandinetti plays with my sister Terry, the Wrobbel girls, and Karen Vinciguerra. Her older sister Joanne is nice. She babysits us on Mom and Dad's rare date nights.

•••

The city of Syracuse officially begins five doors up the street from my house. From that point forward, all of the kids on Kenwick Drive go to a different school. Though we all live within a couple blocks of each other, the Science Club boasts membership from three different schools. Our newest member, Joey Santaro, resides just across the city line. His backyard has the best tree for climbing. It's hard to stay out of it whenever the Club is there, and a tree full of boys, young scientists or not, keeps his Mom in constant distress. Joey's a grade ahead of me and goes to Webster instead of Lyncourt School because of the city line and something called school districts. I live in Lyncourt, and it's about the same distance to Webster and Lyncourt Schools. I keep looking for a line going across the road but never see one.

Mr. and Mrs. Billings live next to the Savastanos, two doors away from us. They're hard to understand, too, just like the Einsteins. Mr. Billings lets us pick fruit from the pear tree in his backyard when it's ripe, and he's friendly to all the kids in the neighborhood. The Savastanos call them Billingsly instead of Billings, but Mr. and Mrs. Billings never correct them. If we hear Mr. Billings playing the violin on his front porch we'll run down to sit on his front steps and listen for a while.

Play us a happy one, Mr. Billings!

Now play a sad one!

That's one's too sad, Mr. Billings—but it's nice!

Play us another one, Mr. Billings—you pick!

Mrs. Billings sits next to him on the porch. They both show genuine interest in our activities.

And vat you children been playing today?

Dos you help your mudders?

Ven the pears ripe, you come and pick, Yah?

Mrs. Billings encourages her husband to keep playing the violin for us. We're lucky that some of the nicest people from Germany moved to Kenwick Drive.

Three doors away and next to the Billings live the Pilons, another family with a girl named Terry. Whenever my Gramma Theresa visits at the same time that Grampa Louis Vinciguerra is next door, there's four Terrys and four Louies on Kenwick Drive within a few houses of each other. I'm the only Lugi, though. I point this out to Leo. He says he's glad and teaches me another lesson—this one's in sarcasm.

•••

CHAPTER FIVE

REVOLTING

Mom calls us home for dinner and we leave Mr. Billings playing the violin on his front porch. Dad's car is in the driveway—he's already drinking a beer in his favorite chair, reading the headlines with his feet propped on the footstool.

Get ready for dinner, kids, Mom says.

We're in a good mood, so we comply without objection or stalling. Dad calls us for dinner and we come the first time we're called. There's something good in that violin music, but Leo can't control himself and plays with the food on his plate. Dad's relieved that Leo gives him an opening to be the Table Monitor. He pounces.

Stop playing with your food, Leo! I work hard to put food on this table, and I had to go hungry when I was growing up, did you know that?

Yes, Dad.

Leo stops playing for two entire minutes and then resumes. He adds chewing food with his mouth open to his repertoire. By now I'm laughing. Dad's not amused, and yells at Leo, who keeps his head down with a sad look on his face.

*You want to be a pig? Well, I'll treat you like a pig
then. Take your plate and eat on the floor under the
table! Go ahead, little pig, get under the table!*

Leo looks confused, but it's obvious that Dad's not
joking. So he begins to slide down the front of his chair
and disappears under the table. Mom protests, but she's
immediately overruled. Terry passes Leo his plate,
knife, fork, and drink. Pigs don't use a napkin, so that
stays on the table.

I'm fascinated with this turn of events and squirm to
catch a glimpse of Leo, now sitting on the floor by my
feet. Dad yells at me to stop looking under the table, but
he doesn't see the pig smiling up at me. I'm dying to join
him. The meal continues awkwardly until we hear a
small voice from under the table.

Can someone pass the peas?

Terry and I start laughing and Mom joins us. To the
little pig's delight, and for once in our lives, Dad gives up
in frustration and huffs off to his chair to finish reading
the paper. After Dad has gotten a safe distance from the
kitchen, I scoot under the table to experience farm life.
To my disappointment Leo doesn't want me around.

●●●

The gang is playing in the Savastanos' backyard, having mixed results avoiding landmines left by old Lassie.
She's a small dog, definitely not a collie, and looks nothing like the Lassie of television fame. She doesn't know
this. For a small dog, she takes a dump like she's a collie,
and it's impossible to avoid her movements in Nicky's
backyard. She provides great clarity in our venue selec-
tion—we don't play a whole lot in a certain backyard.

The fence between ours and the Savastanos' backyard isn't the child-killer type like the Alberts', but it's

not climber friendly, either. A tree in the Savastanos' yard leans toward our house, with a big branch growing across the top of the fence that makes a nice shortcut for impatient boys. Nicky enhances the shortcut by nailing a few boards into the tree that we use as ladder rungs, making it faster to reach our destination.

I'm standing behind Leo at the bottom of the tree in Nicky's yard, waiting for my turn to go over the fence. Leo's parked on the second rung talking with Terry next door. Unbeknownst to him there's a nail in the tree driven halfway home and waiting to catch any part of a hapless tree climber. He tries to make the third rung and the nail goes into his shin. His leg doesn't travel far, and the nail stays put while it rips a nice gash into him.

Blood and screams fill the air. I wince and stagger backward across the minefield, not remembering to look where I'm stepping. I'm sloshing across their back porch when Mrs. Savastano spots me, and I get yelled at for tracking shit across her tiled floor. She's always yelling at people coming in from the backyard to take their shoes off, or at least to check the bottoms before walking on the black and white checkerboard tiles on her enclosed porch. Nicky and Susie mostly ignore her, and the floor shows it. Mrs. Savastano makes me clean her floor anyway.

I arrive home in time to watch Dad hurry Leo off to the doctor's office, where he's introduced to tetanus shots and stitches. I somehow manage to bring remnants of Lassie into our house and I'm catching hell from Mom while Leo's getting his leg sewed up. Mr. Savastano supervises Nicky's removal of the rungs and the nails from the tree and he makes sure that Nicky didn't miss any. After the job is done he gives Nicky a smack for taking his tools without asking him first, and tells him it's his fault that Leo got hurt.

●●●

My big brother's out of commission on the day I need him most. Not long after the tree-nail incident, I'm skipping up the street to Bobby's house and I see two people standing on the sidewalk just past the Vinci- guerras' house. They don't belong there, and my worry radar goes on high alert.

It's Ricky Carapella and his older brother. They live around the corner next to Woodlawn Cemetery. They have a menacing look—I can tell they're up to no good. They size me up from a distance and my disposition makes me an easy mark. Any kid who skips can't be that tough. They beckon, or should I say challenge me to come up a little closer, and being the idiot that I am, I do. I'm the same age as Ricky, but he has a size ad- vantage. The Carapella brothers eye me with contempt. Ricky's brother speaks first while pointing to a crack in the sidewalk.

Cross this line, and you'll have to fight Ricky! Or are you too scared?

Ricky glares at me in ominous silence and I can feel the hairs standing up on the back of my arms. I gulp hard and fight a twitch in my voice to reply.

I would, but my Mom said I can't get dirty before supper.

To the great amusement of the killer Carapella brothers, I ease my way toward the Vinciguerras' drive- way, collecting the shattered remains of my self-respect. Ricky's brother taunts me.

Go see if there's anybody who's brave enough to cross the line!

Ricky chimes in, **Yeah, and don't get dirty, lit- tle baby!**

I slither down the Vinciguerras' driveway and into their backyard. To my relief and embarrassment I find David, Louie, and other assorted Vinciguerras present. I relate my humiliating tale, wishing that I had gone home instead. Louie Vinciguerra is the same age as Ricky's brother, and although David's a year older than Ricky they're the same size, so the rules of fair fight apply. Louie questions me for details.

What did you say after he dared you to cross the line?

I tell him, but take no comfort from the disgusted look on his face. Louie eyes David, ever ready for adventure, and the two of them answer the challenge with passion. I follow at a safe, respectable distance—right behind Bobby and Little Pauly—while performing noticeable examination of the condition of my clothes. If I make it obvious enough, I might convince someone that I'm under strict orders to stay clean.

The two older brothers aren't strangers. They quickly line up the combatants across the crack in the sidewalk from each other. Ricky and David stare each other down, then David spits on the sidewalk to get inside Ricky's head. Ricky's brother again issues the *Cross the line!* challenge. Without hesitating David steps over the line. Ricky looks a bit dismayed, and speaks.

Better ask 'em again, and give 'em a chance to get out of it!

Go ahead, David, Louie encourages, and once more David steps over the line.

The world stands still for a long second. Then the battle erupts, with David and Ricky grabbing, tearing, and pulling at each other before wrestling to the ground. Ricky gains the early advantage and his older brother sneers, *I told you so!* at us while David starts to cry. Louie restrains Bobby and Pauly from entering the fray.

They both want a big piece of Ricky. It's going bad for David, but with three brothers yelling encouragement and better fitness on his side he soon gains the advantage.

Now it's Ricky's turn to cry. Several telling body blows end the affair, and the elder Carapella calls a halt. Ricky's in tears. His brother issues an empty *Wait until next time* threat. They retreat from the battlefield and Louie retorts, *Any time!*

Bobby congratulates David, and Little Pauly hurls assorted mocks, taunts, and insults in his high-pitched voice after the departing Carapellas. The Vinciguerra boys celebrate victory, and Louie, observing me check my pants for stains, casts a final disgusted look my way.

• • •

I'm afraid to fight anyone except Leo and Terry, but I learn that sometimes it hurts more not to. I take a lot of verbal abuse after the *Got to stay clean* story circulates on Kenwick Drive. My resentment builds. I'm arguing with Bobby in his gravel driveway, determined to show the world that I'm no coward. He's younger and a little smaller than me and that helps my courage.

I can take him, I tell myself.

The argument becomes physical after Bobby calls me Lugi Blue Cheese, and ends quickly with a trip-push combination. Bobby runs into his house crying, with scrapes on his leg from the stones in his driveway. I go home to join the other kids playing in our backyard garage. I don't feel sorry for him—he called me a name and got what was coming to him. It's a relief that David isn't there, though I expect him to come over and beat me up after Bobby tells him what happened.

A short time later I hear an unfriendly voice calling for me, but it's not David's. It's Bobby's big, big brother Louie demanding, **Where's Lugi?** I foresee my demise in Louie's menacing gaze. Whatever resides in our attic next to the Halloween masks actually seems preferable. He glares at me and stalks across the backyard garage that would never see a car. His large presence dominates the room—everybody stands clear in awe.

Louie secures both of his hands to the front of my shirt, my feet leave the floor, and he educates me on the dangers of hurting his little brother. I'm frightened and confused at the same time. Between intense premonitions of death, I question how this squares with Louie's eagerness to put David, his other little brother, at risk with Ricky. And why's he getting involved anyway? David is older than me, but closer in age than Louie, with first rights to seek vengeance for Bobby.

My feet long for the earth while I implore Louie with heartfelt assurances of remorse, and vow undying love and concern for his little brother.

I'm sorry, Louie, never again in my life, I swear to God, I'll never touch Bobby again!

Please, Louie, I'm sorry, please, I really like Bobby!

I swear to God, Louie, he's my friend! Is he okay?

Louie, I'm sorry, I didn't mean to hurt him! How's his leg?

Bobby's my best friend, Louie! Please, Louie, please believe me!

Mom arrives to the rescue and my feet regain the garage floor. She's my new best friend and I'll always help her whenever I can, even without being asked.

Mom's maternal instincts spring into high gear at the sight of her youngest being levitated with bad intentions. She starts to rain blows down on Louie while uttering threats of her own. He respectfully accepts her reprimand and soon departs as her final warnings echo across the garage. I want to disappear. Everybody is staring at me while I exhibit various symptoms of acute misfortune and distress.

Later that night, Mr. Vinciguerra stops by to talk with Dad about the legal ramifications of an adult laying hands on another person's child. Dad gets the point, and keeping Mom at bay, he assures him that it won't happen again. The bad feelings dissipate a lot faster for us kids—Bobby and I restart our friendship long before our parents resume cordial relations.

• • •

Another school year begins and we resume carpooling with the Vinciguerra kids. It's a good thing, thawing the cold relationship between our parents after Mom got after Louie, after he got after me, after I pushed Bobby down in his stone driveway and he scraped his leg but good. This year we don't always carpool, though. Sometimes we catch the Centro bus a few blocks away, on Court Street. The familiar yellow school buses don't make runs through our neighborhood to bring kids to Assumption Catholic Academy, so we're compelled to ride the public bus if a parent can't drive.

Mom buys bus tokens for us in advance, and I like the clinking sound of them dropping through the slot next to the driver's seat. Pulling the chord that alerts the driver to stop I like even more. One day on the bus ride home I like it too much. I get carried away—whenever a passenger pulls the chord and it goes beep I give the chord a short pull, too. Every time somebody pulls the chord there's an echo, and if nobody pulls it and the bus goes more than a few blocks I give it pull to make sure that it still works. Before we've gone a mile I happily pull the beep chord repeatedly to the tune of *Shave and a Haircut*. The driver doesn't appreciate my ingenuity or musical talent.

To my horror, he parks the bus, stands up, and glares hatred at me. The passengers watch him stomp down the aisle for a confrontation. He hovers over the seat containing my red face, thoroughly berates me, and lumbers back to the driver's seat at the front of the bus. I suffer extreme embarrassment and want to pull Leo's disappearing act of sliding under the kitchen table.

The four blocks home from the bus stop feel more like four miles—it's a long walk of shame. Leo and Terry delight in my anguish, and let me know that it's not over yet.

Mom's not going to be happy to hear about this, Lugi, and you're gonna be in big trouble, Terry chides.

Yeah, and I wouldn't want to be you after Dad gets home, either!, Leo digs.

But you don't have to tell them, I plead.

I suspect that a secret deal was made between my older brother and sister, because shortly before supper Leo introduces me to the miseries of blackmail and slavery. To secure his silence I'm compelled to do whatever he demands and submit to a life of servitude. He instantly becomes needy, making no pretense of his authority or my predicament.

Lugi, I'm thirsty – get me a glass of water!

Lugi, I left my book upstairs. Go and get it... or shall I tell?

Is there any candy left? Go and look, slave.

*I'm feeling a chill and I want my sweatshirt—go
and get it for me. Right now, too, or else!*

*That's not the one I wanted, slave, put this one back
and get me another.*

What's this? Insolence?

Look at me like that again, Lugi, and you'll regret it!

Two days later I can't endure the fetching any longer
and challenge him to do his worst. He laughs in my face.

You're an idiot, Lugi, I wasn't going to tell on you.

I'm sick of learning things the hard way. I vow he'll
live to regret the day that he made me his slave.

• • •

I love first grade! My new teacher, Sr. Liam, is even
nicer than Mom foretold. Leo and Terry's stories about
the nuns scared me, but Sr. Liam is kind and loving to
everyone. I tell them about her and they're jealous.

I wish I had a teacher like that, Leo whines.

That's what happens to slaveholders, I reflect, and
cherish the moment.

In addition to teaching the first grade class, Sr.
Liam's duties include supervising the school playground—meaning the church parking lot. There's no
grassy play area with a swing set, and we make the most
of the pavement in between parked cars. It gets tricky if
there's a crowded funeral and nowhere to play. The volume of cars coming into and out of the parking lot
worries Sr. Liam, and there are enough close calls to
keep her anxiety level high. By the time afternoon rolls
around she's tired out and needs a break, so she plays
John Philip Sousa marching records. The entire class

marches up and down the aisles between the rows of desks while she catches a second wind, performing deep breathing exercises and imagining quiet streams and gentle breezes in a land with no first graders about to get run over by a car. She rewards well-behaved marchers with colored stars that stick to their shirt collars. Everybody wants one. I puff out my chest when I march by her desk, hoping to win a star sticker. The chest puffing works! I get two stars for my collar, one green and a prized gold one.

I want Dad to see the shiny stars on me when he gets home from work so I keep my school clothes on after school. Leo says I'm a show-off but I don't care, it's my turn to teach him something. It's a lesson on revenge, and it's best served cold.

Dad comes home from work and he likes my stickers. Leo frowns with jealousy. Then Dad says his other famous word, second only to *Geeez.* He takes a deep breath and utters the other long word that takes time to come out, and ends with a slight gasp.

Weh-hll...!

Ha! Another blow to the slaveholder. Best of all, I make him know that it's me that's doing it to him. Ha!

• • •

The next day in school starts out with Music class and it's my favorite, because we all get to sing in chorus. I've got a decent singing voice and hit the high notes with the best of them. Sr. Liam uses a pitch pipe to let us hear the key we're to sing in, and we commence with an old standard, The Erie Canal Song.

I've got a mule and her name is Sal
Fifteen miles on the Erie Canal

She's a good old worker and a good old pal
Fifteen miles on the Erie Canal

Get up there mule, here comes a lock
We'll make Rome 'bout six o'clock
Every inch of the way we know
From Albany to Buffalo

Low bridge, everybody down
Low bridge, we're comin' to a town
And you'll always know your neighbor
And you'll always know your pal
If ya ever navigated on the Erie Canal

The day is off to a good start. I'm anxious to win more star stickers... but I get sick all over the classroom floor instead. My stomach feels like it's inside out. And I can't get the Erie Canal Song out of my head. I'm starting to panic about having fifteen miles to go, but Sr. Liam assures me that the worst is over and she runs to get the janitor. The sight, sound, and smell repulse my classmates, especially the girls. Everyone backs away from my pallid, green-tinged face and the multicolored mess on the floor.

Ewwww! Yeuch! Gahh!

Marybeth is the farthest one away, and she already hasn't wanted to talk to me since Kindergarten. Sister Liam returns with the janitor, who wheels in a large canister on a dolly. He knows the drill, having had years of experience cleaning up after kids who threw up on the floor. He opens the canister and scoops out a large amount of something I've never seen. He sprinkles it all over the mess and puts the lid back on. The boys become interested and slowly approach to see what's happening. The girls stay distant but stretch their necks to satisfy their curiosity.

I'll be back shortly, the janitor tells Sr. Liam, and he wheels the dolly back out the door.

Thank you, she replies, and whispers to me that she's going across the hall to ask someone in the office to call my Mom to come pick me up.

Everyone return to your seats, I'll be back in one minute!

When class resumes, the metamorphosis happening on the floor becomes a distraction. The sprinkle stuff is slowly absorbing everything and it's turning into thick orange blobs. Janitors like it because it makes the clean-up easier. I ponder whether he'll return with a shovel, a dustpan, or both.

The transformation process makes it impossible for Sister to teach, commanding more attention from the class than her lesson. Many classmates now appreciate the bile interruption, and several sitting nearby thank me for getting sick. Once again I find that God works in mysterious ways. I try to catch Marybeth's eye.

•••

I'm allowed to stay home sick the next day and find it rather nice having Leo and Terry at school and just me and Mom at home.

What do you want for breakfast, Lugi?

Soft boiled eggs in a cuppie, Mom!

I get to say cuppie instead of cup if nobody but Mom can hear me—especially not the guys in the Science Club.

Okay, she says. *Why don't you watch TV and lay on the couch with a blanket?*

Okay, Mom!

Staying home sick from school gets better by the minute.

I check the three channels that work and the one that almost does, but to my dismay the best thing on is The Magic Toy Shop. I kind of like it but it's mostly for girls and little kids. I never connected with Eddie Flum Dum, Merilee, or the Play Lady, and Twinkles the Clown gives me nightmares. I do like Mr. Trolley, though—especially when he says, *Ladies and Gentlemen, and puppy dogs, too...*

After breakfast I'm excited to watch one of my favorites, Captain Kangaroo. I like all of the characters on this one—the Captain, Mr. Green Jeans, Mr. Moose, Bunny Rabbit, Dancing Bear, Grandfather Clock, and the others. The show even has a cartoon of Tom Terrific. I'm on the edge of my seat, waiting for Mr. Moose to dump ping pong balls on the Captain's head.

Mom cleans up the kitchen, walks into the living room, and changes the channel.

I want to watch Ladies Day, she says.

But, Mom...

But nothing, Lugi, you're supposed to be sick—so go to bed and read a book.

•••

Halloween approaches and I need to re-inspect the Halloween costumes in our scary attic. I con Leo into helping me drag the costume boxes out, still convinced that something unseen lives there in the dark waiting to catch me alone. The boxes include plastic masks in the likeness of John F. and Jackie Kennedy. They came from Aunt Rosemary's involvement in the local Democratic Party. During the 1960 Presidential campaign she organized the local chapter of the Kennedy Girls, and recruited Terry and my cousin Mary Anne, who became *Little* Kennedy Girls. We all like the beaming white smiles on the Kennedy masks. I wish that we still had the costumes that came with them. The smiling masks are a little eerie, too, because I know what happened to him a few years after he became President.

I'm busy admiring the Kennedy masks until I sense that my

Aunt Ro with JFK

bladder's about to burst. I run downstairs, mask in hand, and in my haste I leave the bathroom door open, doing the pee dance in front of the toilet. I can't pee and hold the mask at the same time, so I instinctively put the mask on and go about my business. Being a boy, and naturally competitive, I back away a couple steps to practice my aim and work on my arc and distance. With training in progress, I hear a noise from the next room and turn John Kennedy's face in time to spot my brother. I wave to him in Presidential style. He's a little shocked at first, not expecting to see John F. Kennedy going pee, but to my delight he bursts out laughing. I'm so pleased with the outcome that the following day I hold my pee so he gets to see Jackie Kennedy repeat the performance.

Leo tells the boys about the recent sightings of Kennedys going pee on Kenwick Drive and everybody laughs. Well, everyone except Nicky.

He's not dead, you know, Nicky states with matter-of-fact confidence.

What do you mean, he's not dead? Everybody knows he's dead!

That's just what the government wants you to believe, but he's really alive somewhere and they won't let anybody know where he is.

Nicky, you're crazy, I say, and instinctively brace myself for a punch.

The boys take my side in the argument, but Nicky's the alpha male and never cares much about the odds. Without a means to settle the dispute it looks like a stalemate, until David suggests a solution that we all agree to. His idea involves using the all-knowing Ouija board to consult the great beyond, and because it's the Halloween season, so much the better.

It's kind of like a duel, us against Nicky, and the first order of business is choice of weapons. David and Nicky both have Ouija boards and both claim that theirs is better. Because Nicky's outnumbered we allow him to choose, and he departs to retrieve the home board. To maintain fair play we insist that the séance be held in the Vinciguerras' garage.

Everyone's excited at the prospect of terror, and David says he'll get a candle and matches. The Science Club piles into the Vinciguerras' garage—me, Leo, Nicky, Joey, David, Bobby, and even Little Pauly. We place the Ouija board on an old card table and take our places, with Nicky at the head. David lights the candle, Bobby pulls the garage door closed, and I begin to shit my pants in the darkened garage.

Multiple pokings, proddings, and whispered jokes break out, but Nicky takes control. In a stern voice he tells everybody to knock it off and shut up. A final

Ooooohh or two escape, and Joey suggests that we join hands to make connection with the spirits. We do so, and Nicky begins in a hushed, chanting tone, the kind spoken only when consulting the spirit world.

Oh Weegie, he starts, and at least three people can't contain their laughter. Nicky's pissed.

Knock it off! You just don't want to find out that I'm right!

Okay, Nicky, we'll stop, please start over!

The laughter fades and Nicky starts again.

Oh Weegie, he repeats, but achieves the same results.

That's it! I'm leaving, he fumes, and makes his way to depart.

No wait, don't go, we won't laugh anymore!

No, I'm leaving, he says in frustration, one hand on the rope to pull the garage door open.

Aw, c'mon Nicky, let's try again. We won't laugh anymore!

*Alright, but if anybody starts laughing again I'm leaving and I'm **not** coming back!*

The group somehow manages to control themselves, and a serious mood overcomes the candlelit garage. Nicky starts again.

Oh Weegie, he chants, and pauses to look around to see if anybody's laughing before he continues. It's unfortunate for Nicky that he sometimes mispronounces words.

Oh Weegie, is John F. Kennedy a vesh-able?

The spirits immediately answer in the chorus of five voices laughing hysterically, including mine, although I'm still scanning the darkness for movement. Nicky abruptly departs, overturning the card table and candle in the process. He doesn't look back. We squint against the sudden daylight from the open garage door. We all watch him storm away down the driveway, which only adds to the comedy. Impersonating Nicky's voice, David calls after him.

Oh Weegie, you forgot your board!

We all laugh again, and Leo says we're lucky that we didn't get killed in a fire after the candle got knocked over. I decide that it's best to avoid Nicky for a while. It's not until after we go trick-or-treating with him on Halloween that he's back to his old self.

The Kennedy Girls in 1960

•••

CHAPTER SIX

NOW *THAT'S* CATHOLIC

It's December twenty-fourth, and I'm in first grade, so that means I'm old enough for altar boy duty at Midnight Mass. The entire school at Assumption Catholic participates in some fashion, with no exceptions. Smartly attired altar boys line the rows of stairs leading to the altar. We're arranged by school grade and according to height. Girls aren't allowed on the altar, but they're in the procession. They fill the first few rows of pews closest to the altar, right behind the nuns and priests not participating in the ceremony.

The church service includes members of the Syracuse Symphony Orchestra, a full choir, and the Knights of Columbus, who frame the procession aisle in full dress uniform, including their shiny swords. A heavy scent of burning incense fills the church, adding to the pageantry.

Prior to going to church, our Italian Christmas Eve feast includes plenty of seafood: raw clams, steamed clams, clams casino, shrimp cocktail, shrimp scampi, and fried calamari. Gramma's here, so the meal includes a macaroni dish—this time it's linguini with mussels in a tomato-garlic sauce. There's a big pot of meatballs, sausage, and pork, and don't forget the fresh Italian bread from Columbus Bakery. Aunt Ro makes a cheesecake for dessert, and there's fried dough strips coated with honey and powdered sugar. Gramma's famous tray of Christmas cookies completes the menu—arguably the best part.

Midnight Mass lasts for more than an hour. Mom wants us all to try to get some sleep after dinner so we'll be able to stay awake later on tonight. The Visconti kids include two altar boys and a procession girl, Dad's an usher, and Mom, Aunt Ro, Gramma, and Grampa attend the mass—so our whole family will be up very late. Dad takes his favorite chair, and it's first come, first served for the remaining seats in the living room. Mom hustles us off to bed. She wants to save time getting us ready to go out later.

Leo and Lugi, don't bother putting your pajamas on, you'll just take them off in a couple hours to get dressed again.

Okay, Mom!

I never got in bed without my PJs before. The sheets feel cold and kind of weird, but it's fun. I see that Leo is affected the same way in his twin bed next to mine, and we start thrashing about and laughing. Mom's down the hall in Terry's room giving instructions, and she hears us.

You boys get to sleep or you won't stay awake during mass. If either one of you falls asleep on the altar, boy, will you get it! You better not embarrass me!

Okay, Mom!

It's a safe bet that at least one of the young altar boys won't make it through the entire mass, compelling a priest or an older boy to carry him off. It's easier to stay awake for the standing and sitting parts of the mass, but during the long stretch of kneeling down it's a lot harder.

Half-way through the mass I'm kneeling and feel my eyelids start to close while my chin starts a southerly descent. Suddenly my head snaps upward, reviving me to a degree. The smell of the incense is stupefying. I glance around the church and observe other heads nodding everywhere, and it makes me tired by association. I spot Mom frowning at me, and that wakes me up again. I shouldn't look behind me at the people in church—they even told us that during rehearsals—but I can't help it. I need a distraction to keep me awake. So I start counting the number of people asleep in church. An old man starts snoring and his wife elbows him right in the gut.

I'm in the second row from the top and observe an altar boy in the first row suffering from extreme head nods. This provides a jolt of energy. I whisper to Joe Callahan, who's kneeling next to me because we're the same height.

Hey Joe, look at Rich, he's falling asleep.

Yeah, I see him.

I don't think he's gonna make it.

Shhhh!

Talking on the altar is something else that we're not supposed to do. It's a mortal sin, worse than turning around and counting sleepers.

Rich is kneeling right in front of a podium decorated with an ornamental wreath and his head nods lengthen with each occurrence. He finally succumbs to slumber, face first, and the microphone on the lectern amplifies the thud of his head hitting the podium right under the holiday wreath. Lucky for Rich that his guardian angel turns his head so he doesn't get a bloody nose upon landing—but he's lying there in a daze, covered in pine needles. A nearby priest comes to the rescue and carries him off the altar, still half asleep. All of the altar boys and everyone who's still awake in church watch with great interest. The Pastor pauses, waiting for the distraction to end.

I'm on full alert for the remainder of the mass. Rich falling asleep gives his fellow altar boys a much-needed shot of adrenaline. After mass I see him in the sacristy behind the altar—wide awake, a big smile on his face and very glad to see us. He isn't embarrassed at all. I admire him for that—and for helping me stay out of trouble with Mom.

• • •

Passing snowplows leave the deepest and heaviest snow, and it's fun to build snow forts and dig tunnels by the side of the road. During the winter on Kenwick Drive you can tell which families have boys, because there's always a snow fort on their front lawn. Opposing forts within firing range of each other decide the location for snow ball fights, and some of the nicer neighbors without boys let us build auxiliary forts on their lawns, too. Capturing enemy forts adds to the fun. Leo and I make twin forts in our front yard, connected by a tunnel through which we run supplies like icicles, snowballs, snacks, and water. Icicles are illegal weapons, and are kept only as a deterrent.

Joey comes to our house from up the street, and the once dreaded Ricky of *Cross the line* infamy has become a friend, too. The Vinciguerras join in, and a decent snowball fight ensues. The battle continues through the afternoon. Mom yells out the door that it's starting to get dark and we have to come in soon. There isn't a clear winner so we plan a big battle for tomorrow. We decide to pour water on our snowballs so they'll freeze overnight.

The battle resumes the next day. But it's not long before several combatants run home crying after getting hit in the face by an iceball. Until now, only icicles have been outlawed by the Kenwick Geneva Convention—but now we declare iceballs illegal, along with gassing snow tunnels with farts. This last, to no avail. Leo gasses me without remorse in our own tunnel, and I become the first casualty of friendly fire in the war. I should have known better than to follow him too closely in the tunnel when there was no room to turn around. He knows that he farted, and after hearing my shrieks I believe that he deliberately slows down to savor the full effect.

Ughhh! It stinks! Ewww! Keep going! Gahhh! Why'd you slow down?

Luckily the gas doesn't cause the tunnel to collapse and bury us both, but he's quite pleased with himself when we emerge. In a rage, I go for his throat. The enemy begins to pelt us with snowballs. Only the thought of losing the battle makes me stop—well, that and repeatedly getting thrown into the snow. We lose the battle and I tell him it's his fault—but he looks like he already won.

It's snowing the next day. The Wrobbel girls come outside to shovel, and begin filling in the South Fort. I'm furious and yell at them.

Throw the snow on one side of your driveway, like we do!

They both ignore me and Diane shovels me in where I stand. They're lucky it's a cold day and lousy packing for snowballs. Diane Wrobbel's four years older than me. She could easily destroy me, and enjoys hearing stories from Terry about the times she beat me up. Snowballs provide a means for me to retaliate from a safe distance, but the poor packing leaves me resigned to calling names and making faces. The shoveled snow continues to fill in the fort despite my best efforts. But at least my feet stay dry, because Mom always makes me wear plastic Wonderbread bags over my shoes before I put on my black rubber boots that buckle in the front.

Winter's almost over. One day the worst casualty in the snowball wars happens on our front lawn. It's late winter—or early spring, by the calendar—and the snow forts have all melted away. There's an abundance of ice from the melting snow that refreezes during the night. Everyone agrees to allow the use of iceballs. The battle commences at close range, with no cover for either side. A scream goes out whenever an iceball connects with its target. Bobby's on my side and gets pinned down while he's out in the open. He starts to cry from getting hit repeatedly. I can't just leave him there, so I play the hero and stand in front of him.

Joey doesn't care about the hero nonsense, and lets fly with a good one that catches me high on the forehead. It doesn't hurt badly, but it's scary the way the blood flows down my face and into the snow, so I instinctively start crying. My onetime nemesis, big Louie Vinciguerra, hears my cries and comes down to see what's happening. He sees the blood and carries me inside without even looking disgusted at me. Dad takes me to the doctor's office and I get two stitches and a tetanus shot. On the drive back home I recall how Louie helped me. It's worth the price of the iceball and the stitches that followed.

•••

I don't believe in the Easter Bunny any more, but I still look forward to Easter baskets filled with goodies. It's kind of like Halloween in the springtime. We badly need another overdose of chocolate, and our Easter baskets provide us with a good fix. It's hard to wait for Easter Sunday and getting our baskets of chocolate, but this year Mom surprises us the week before Easter with a real live white rabbit. We name him Fluffy and commence fighting over who gets to hold him. Dad makes a cage for Fluffy. Nobody's happy after Mom informs us that he's going to live in the cellar. I start peppering her with questions, trying to change her mind.

Won't he get scared being down there all alone at night, Mom?

No.

How do you know?

Would you like to sleep down there with him?

Yes!

No. I was only joking.

There's room by the front door, can we keep him there?

No.

I notice Mom starting to step toward me like she did the day she chased Terry around the dining room table. I stop asking questions.

I really love the rabbit, and can't wait to get home from school every day to play with him. I like to lay down on the couch and put him on my stomach, where he receives many hugs and enough baby talk to make Leo and Terry want to puke.

It's a sunny day, and we bring Fluffy into our backyard to let him feel the grass under his feet for a change instead of plywood. Our friends join us and we all enjoy watching Fluffy hopping around. Leo grabs a clothes basket to throw over Fluffy in case he gets any ideas about escape.

I'll put some turds in their Easter baskets.

Then we see the cat. It's all hunched up and ready to pounce on poor Fluffy. I'm screaming at the cat and throwing anything I can get my hands on. Terry sees the danger and scoops Fluffy up off the ground and heads inside.

Mrs. Wilson happens to be in her backyard. She becomes disturbed by the commotion, the objects flying over her fence, and whatever she happens to be drinking. Flying objects, kids, and noise aren't her favorite cocktail.

Youse kids! Hey, youse kids!

Yes, Mrs. Wilson?

Youse kids! Knock off that racket! Which one of youse threw stuff into my yard?

I did, Mrs. Wilson. I was trying to protect my rabbit.

My direct answer confuses Mrs. Wilson. She can only focus on the last word I said.

Rabbit? I don't want your father! Youse kids better mind me!

Now it's my turn to be confused. I don't know what to say and she sees me scratching my leg.

What's wrong boy, you got itchy pants?

Everybody laughs at me, but I'm not interested in arguing with Mrs. Wilson so I leave her there to go check on Fluffy. I commence baby talking to him. Terry huffs off in disgust.

Mom and Dad aren't pet people. Fluffy departs a few weeks later. It's a sad day for me, but Mom says that he's going to live on a farm where he can play in the grass every day. Leo says the farmer is going to fatten him up and Terry adds that they're going to eat Fluffy, too. I'm gawking at Mom, who doesn't contradict them once, and they all have a good laugh.

I'm still distraught over Fluffy when the other shoe drops. Leo and Terry need to relieve their boredom, so they target my favorite stuffed animal—Smokey the Bear—who I sleep with every night. I'm very attached to Smokey, they both know it, and together they plot against me. It's lunchtime in our kitchen and I'm summoned to partake. Leo and Terry look at each other and try to suppress giggles. Mom tries to act nonchalant. I detect something amiss, but remain clueless. Leo looks at me and speaks.

Lugi, Mom bought some good popsicles. Want one?

Okay!

Upon opening the freezer I find Smokey inside with a clothesline tied around his neck.

Smokey!!

I scream in horror, but their laughter is louder.

• • •

The Easter Sunday mass at Assumption church rivals that of Christmas Eve. Once again all of the altar boys participate. Rehearsals include practicing the part where we kneel down on the stairs for a long time. Today it's unusually lengthy. I'm feeling the fatigue, and lean over to whisper to the boy next to me.

Hey Joe, are you getting tired?

I've heard that whispering on the altar is one of the greatest sins known to man, and now an elderly nun demonstrates the consequences to me. Her black-framed visage swoops down on me. She utters threats about talking on the altar and drags me off the stairs by one of my ears. The entire cast of altar boys, priests, and bystanders witness the act of discipline. Nobody says or does anything. Apparently it's acceptable to terrorize a six-year-old on the altar if you're teaching him that talking on the altar is a sin. None of the priests, nuns, or other adults come to my aid. I sit crying, shivering, and alone in a small room behind the altar, where she leaves me, telling me to pray to God for forgiveness for the remainder of the rehearsal. An eternity passes before it comes to an end. Every boy receives a big green candy sucker on a stick. Every boy except for one, that is. Not satisfied that I had sufficiently paid for my sin, the old nun rips the sucker out of my hand and shrieks,

None for you!!

She sounds just like the Wicked Witch of the West, and looks like her, too, dressed all in black, except that her face is pale white instead of green. She's a living terror and a six-year-old's nightmare, all rolled into one.

The next day in school I'm called to the front of the class by Sister Liam. I expect further public humiliation, because now everyone knows of the great sin I committed. I try to ignore her but she persists.

I'm waiting, young man!

I lower my head and make my way to her desk, bracing myself for a smack because I reflected poorly on the first grade class. She opens her desk and I'm waiting for the ruler to come out. Instead she extracts the big green candy sucker taken from me the day before. To my amazement she gives me a big, long hug for all to see and whispers to me.

I think this is yours! I'm sorry about what happened yesterday, and I think you're a good boy.

Her act of kindness restores my faith in God and man. I get back to wishing for my Easter basket.

Near the end of the school year, the first grade receives several impromptu visits from our principal, Sr. Seraphica. Her office is across the hall from our classroom, and she tells Sr. Liam that the first grade kids cheer her up. I didn't know she needed cheering up— she's a kind, gentle, loving person and smiles a lot. The kids I see crying on the way into or coming out of her office probably encountered a mean nun or actually did something bad. I hear lots of stories about mean nuns, but apart from being attacked on the altar, so far I've experienced the opposite.

Sr. Seraphica pops into our classroom at different times and sits in an empty chair at the back of the room without saying a word. She exchanges smiles with Sr. Liam and class goes on as if she wasn't even there. I can't help turning around to look at her, but she just smiles and points her index finger down and makes a circling motion indicating for me to turn around. After a little while, I hear the door open and close, and she's back in her office across the hall.

•••

CHAPTER SEVEN

KENWICK SKIRMISHES

It's early morning and Leo's dreaming of putting hairnets on Dad's skull again. I'm lying awake in bed and watch him stir from his slumbers in the bed next to mine. His eyes blink and he looks at me with determination.

Let's go down and fix Dad's head, Lugi.

No response necessary, I slip out of bed and follow him in great anticipation. Leo's not a morning person. He wakes up with his system on autopilot. We've pulled this stunt before, but it's always exciting to stalk a giant in his own castle.

Once again we tiptoe down the hallway. Leo gives me dirty looks on the stairs—as if I want them to squeak, or something. I take the observation post outside our parents' bedroom and watch him follow the familiar script.

Open headboard drawer and extract hairnet—check.

Walk around bed, not waking sleepers—check.

Stand over Dad and attach hairnet to skull—almost.

Dad's lying there motionless and Leo stands over him with the hairnet nearing its destination. Then one of Dad's eyes pops open. A Cyclops gazes up at Leo, who begins to tremble, drool, and stutter. Dad doesn't move and Leo escapes with his life, running at the speed of light.

A few days later I still want to alter Dad's hairdo, but Leo says he won't risk it so soon. His recent near-death experience has taken the adventure out of him, and it's left to me to settle the score. Dad's asleep in his favorite chair, his bare feet propped on the footstool and his legs crossed at the ankles. I'm staring at his big toe pointing up to the heavens. It seems comparable in size to my entire foot. The big toe closest to the ceiling acts like a beacon, calling to me and giving me instructions at the same time. It tells me that my socks and sneakers belong on Dad's big toes, and while I comply Leo and Terry watch and laugh. I tie the sneaker laces so they look nice and neat. We pursue other amusements, laughing occasionally whenever we catch a glimpse of the spectacle, leaving Dad snoring away in his chair. Mom likes practical jokes as long as she's not the victim, and condones our mischief with a smirk.

Toe sneakers provide the perfect backdrop for one of Dad's friends to pay him an unexpected visit. His buddy enters, and Dad begins to revive from his lethargy, feet on footstool, legs crossed at the ankles, big toes wearing socks and sneakers. He doesn't know what everyone's laughing at. He feigns a tired smile at his friend. His eyes focus on the toe costume and he's not smiling anymore, but his friend laughs harder.

Is that a new style you're wearing? Where's your other eight sneakers?

It's no mystery who wears that shoe size. Dad casts one of his freezing glares my way. A dire fate awaits me after Dad's friend departs, and I pray for Mom to ask him to move into the spare room. My prayer is answered in another way—I'm ever so glad that Dad and his friend decide to start drinking.

Do you want a cold Genny, Dad? I can get one for your friend, too!

Dad's in a good mood from the unexpected visit and the cold Genesees. After his friend departs he's forgotten that everyone laughed at him for wearing my socks and sneakers on his big toes pointing up to the heavens.

I feel safe again and tell Leo next time it's his turn.

• • •

It's not fair that Leo's so big for his age, worse yet because he's two years older and I'm compelled to live with him. Other boys on our street suffer my fate and we don't have much of a chance in taking him on, no matter how much we want to. Crazy Nicky's the only one who's strong enough to take him in a fight, but the two of them get along famously. Leo just trounced me again and I appeal to Nicky for justice, but he just laughs and tells me to fight my own battles. Thanks for nothing, Mr. Science Club President.

It's hard for David Vinciguerra to accept Leo's size advantage, because he's the same age as Leo but he's not much bigger than I am. He can take me in a fight, but Leo—well, forget it. David likes to be right and win arguments, but it's unhealthy for him, especially having Leo as a nemesis.

Leo and David quarrel on our front lawn. It becomes physical and very unfortunate for David. I'm rooting for him, wanting to see Leo get his for a change, but once again it's not happening. Like any one of my fights with Leo, David's mad and Leo isn't, which only makes him madder still. Leo utters his famous final words.

You'd better stop!

His unfortunate opponent, usually me, often ignores the warning. In this case it's David. He finds himself thrown over Leo's shoulder and carried across the street. Their destination becomes clear when Leo approaches the Rellis' front yard with his cargo.

Mrs. Relli's landscaping includes several immaculately trimmed shrubs, the kind with lots of little red berries and even more sharp little thorns that we call prickers. As they get close to the pricker bushes, David figures out what's coming and begins to kick and scream and curse, but all to no avail—into Mrs. Relli's pricker bushes he goes. Leo's back across the street before David extracts himself, encountering countless prickers along the way. I don't know which hurts more—getting thrown into prickers with force or slowly getting yourself out from the bottom of a pricker bush.

David's already angry, but the encounter with the bush full of berries and prickers helps him achieve Frenzy level on the Kenwick Rage Scale. He throws caution to the wind and attacks Leo in a fury, but only ends up kicking and screaming on Leo's shoulders and getting tossed into the pricker bushes again.

After a few iterations of *Let's Throw David Into the Pricker Bushes,* Mrs. Relli's shrubs begin to take David's body form. David looks like he did the time his Mom rescued him from the Alberts' fence. It's hard to tell if it's blood or berry juice leaving the red streaks all over his skin and clothes—probably both. Lucky for David, his Mom hears his cries and calls him home in time to prevent another trip to the bushes and the hundreds of prickers. He's beginning to know them all by name.

I watch him walk home and little bush leaves, berries, and prickers fall away from his clothes, leaving a trail behind him. He's crying, shaking, and uttering incoherent threats at Leo, looking like a human collage of dirt, grass stain, berry juice, and blood. He's covered with pricker bush scratches from head to toe. I expect to see his impersonation of the Mummy again before long. To David's credit and Leo's relief, David doesn't get his big brother Louie to pound Leo. I feel a bit cheated.

It's admirable, no doubt. But I would have.

•••

Dad the Table Monitor makes getting through supper an adventure. He keeps me on my toes. I'm aware that he makes me eat everything on my plate, but having eyes bigger than my stomach, I often still suffer the consequences. Many meals end with me scowling at the table until the food on my plate disappears, or worse yet, not getting to go outside to play afterward. I find this especially cruel on pleasant evenings like tonight. I hear the kids outside having a good old time without me.

Where's Lugi?

He can't come out.

Why not? Did you have squash again?

Nah, no squash, but he didn't eat everything on his plate.

Oh, too bad—my Dad just tells me that I can't have any dessert. Let's go play!

I'm listening from my bedroom window, and commence scheming how to thwart the Table Monitor. An idea comes to me in a flash of brilliance. The next night I execute my plan. Instead of loading my plate with everything, I now eat dinner one item at a time. The strategy achieves the desired results—at the end of the meal there's never more than one item to contend with. I improvise and limit the volume, too, along with the associated risk. I'm quite pleased with myself, and even more amazed that my maneuver isn't overruled by Dad the Table Monitor. He does insist that I eat the vegetables before the meat. My brother Leo, the junior analyst, scoffs at me and asks what I'll do if Mom serves vegetable soup. I wait until supper ends and we're alone to tell him where he can put his bowl of soup, one vegetable at a time.

•••

I'm doing a great job finishing everything on my plate and I'll get to go outside and play after supper. The birds sing and the sun shines on Kenwick Drive. Or so I think. After the meal concludes I once again find myself listening to the kids playing outside from my bedroom window.

Courtesy of the Table Monitor, I learn of new violations punishable by grounding – all unrelated to food. Tonight's crimes include uncleanliness, mispronouncing words, and disrespect to your elders.

Dad scrubs thoroughly after coming home from the construction site, so he's easily riled if we come to the dinner table with a dirty face or hands. Tonight I'm guilty on both counts. We say grace and Dad notices my dirty face.

Go wash your face, Louis, you're thilthy!

Dad doesn't say filthy, he says thilthy. Nobody knows why.

Okay, Dad. Mom, can you let me out, please?

I'm sitting next to the wall with my back to the refrigerator and Mom needs to get up in order for me to go to the bathroom. After I return she stands up again for me to get back to my seat. I reach for the first vegetable, using the proven *one at a time* technique. As I'm reaching, Dad sees the dirt on the back of my hands.

Look at those hands, Louis! I thought I told you to wash!

I did, Dad. I don't eat with that side of my hands, though.

Don't you get smart with me, Mister!
Now get going!

Yes, Dad. Mom, can you let me out, please?

Mom gets up again and tells me I'd better wash my hands right this time. I wash both sides of my hands, and when I return Mom's compelled to get up again. I consume my first vegetable but I'm still hungry and reach for the next item. The Table Monitor notices something else.

Louis, what did you get into today? The back of your neck is thilthy!

Sorry, Dad. Mom, can you let me out, please?

No! *Can I eat my dinner in peace? Leo, I'll make him take a bath after we're done!*

Dad's about to argue with her, but she turns on me. She delivers a smack that doesn't hurt me, but it appeases Dad. Leo and Terry start laughing. Mom continues.

That's enough, you two! Now let's change the subject, shall we? Leo, what happened at work today?

Dad begins with his famous long word with the gasp at the end.

We-eh-hll...! Today the guys were talking about all the baloney going on in Hong Hong, and...

Mom interrupts him. *Where did you say?*

Hong Hong.

Never heard of it. Where's Hong Hong?

Leo Junior, the analyst, intervenes.

Do you mean Hong Kong, Dad?

That's what I said, Hong Hong. So anyways they're saying this baloney going on over there in Hong Hong will start happening here soon and...

Mom interrupts him again.

Stop saying Hong Hong, Leo, it's Hong Kong!

Why do I bother saying anything? All I'm good for is paying the bills!

No, you give me agita, too!

I don't want my parents to argue, and try to help.

Dad, I bet the people are pretty thilthy over there in Hong Hong, don't you think?

Leo and Terry laugh again. Dad's fuming. I'm sent to my room for the night, but at least I don't have to take a bath.

● ● ●

There's a kickball game happening right in front of our house that includes all of the Kenwick kids, both boys and girls. Everybody's here—even the Gaciochs get a reprieve to play with us. My sister Terry's a girly-girl and she's not into competition sports, but she likes kickball. The other girls on our street like playing kickball, too. An intense match is arranged without any controversy.

From time to time someone's pride gets hurt, along with their face, when a base runner gets put out by an aggressive defender. The usual interruptions occur, too, whenever a car goes by. Somebody yells out **CAR!** and the teams retire to either side of the road, waiting for it to pass by. A good street game seems to attract cars from miles around. We shake our heads in frustration—the traffic is so light most of the time.

Now it's Terry's turn to kick. The defenders take to the ready, the base runners tense, the pitcher rolls the ball toward her. She misses the ball and kicks the road instead, screaming and collapsing to the ground in pain. All of the girls on both teams run to her aid—even some of the boys on her team gather around behind them. The other boys freeze in silence and disbelief that someone could actually miss the ball and kick the road.

Mom's on the scene in a flash and runs to Terry's aid. It's no coincidence. Terry's her favorite. Mom watches the kickball games from our porch, but only when Terry plays. Her youngest feels he's a victim of neglect. Assisted by the neighborhood girls, Mom hauls Terry into our house. The drama and hysterics echo up and down Kenwick Drive.

IT HURTS! I BROKE MY FOOT!
I CAN'T WALK! HELP ME – IT HURTS!

Mom gets on board the panic train. In great distress she cries aloud,

What are we going to do?

I don't know if she's addressing Dad or the Almighty, but Dad's the only one visible, so I figure it must be him. He answers in a deadpan voice from his favorite chair.

Better call a big toe truck.

Mom's not amused by Dad's caring display of empathy, but to his credit he immediately brings Terry to the Doctor's office. She hasn't broken her foot, just her big toe, but I guess that's close enough. Terry eventually regains the use of her big toe and the ability to walk, but she never plays kickball in the street again.

I begin to understand which side of the family my sense of humor comes from.

• • •

CHAPTER EIGHT

GREATEST HITS

This summer the Science Club adds several butterfly nets to its arsenal. The number of captured butterflies climbs dramatically. It's not difficult to improve on—before that we caught very few using the metal coffee can and plastic lid method. Butterflies top the prize list in the Science Club, especially colorful monarchs or yellow and black swallowtails. We look hard for caterpillars and cocoons, too. Though we manage to hatch several cocoons, nobody's ever witnessed it happen live inside one of our incubator jars.

Leo's in charge of putting the best of the best on display in a special glass case, their wings fully extended. It's fun to stalk and catch butterflies, but I want to put them in the glass case and Leo won't let me. Fine then. If I can't put butterflies in the case then I'll nail bugs to ceiling tiles when nobody's looking. I defy Club protocol, refusing to wait for approval from Science Club President Nicky or Chief Know-It-All Leo. I grab a ceiling tile, a bug jar, hammer and nails, and commence bug mounting.

Things proceed well until I focus on a recently captured wasp. He's in a jar without air holes in the lid, but I know that he's still alive because I can see that he's still moving, albeit slowly. I give the jar a good shake, and figure he's dead or dazed enough that I can continue. I open the lid and pour him into my hands, ready to start nailing.

Leo approaches and catches me red-handed in the act of unauthorized bug impalement. His loud protests distract me for a moment. I forget that there's a live wasp between my fingers. The wasp begins to recover and he's moving with greater animation than a dazed twitch. Leo sights the movement and takes a step backward. I begin to freak out. Instinct tells me to throw the wasp and run, but instead I reach down with my other hand and pull him in two. Leo is stunned by this heroic action, and stammers.

Y-you... just killed a wasp with your bare hands!

Yes, I did! I just killed a wasp with my bare hands!

Soon, other Club members start filing back into headquarters. I become the topic of conversation.

Did you hear Lugi killed a wasp with his bare hands?

No way, he's lying. Did anyone see him do it?

Yeah, Leo saw him—he's the one who told me!

President Nicky examines the two halves of the wasp, believes Leo's account, and declares that I'm the bravest man in the Science Club. It's the proudest moment of my life. I killed a wasp with my bare hands, and I'm the bravest one in our club.

There's a down side that accompanies this title, and it soon becomes obvious. Whenever Club business requires a volunteer, or an idiot, who better to ask than the bravest one in the club? My proven courage in wasp killing allows me to resolve a myriad of issues like:

How deep is that puddle?

Is it safe to stand on that branch?

Do you think the dog is friendly?

Who's going to stand up to the bully?

At the least sign of hesitation I'm told if I don't do it I'm no longer the bravest one in the club. At a young age I learn the dangers of vanity, and what it means to take one for the team.

•••

It's a beautiful summer day—a great time to try smoking. We temporarily move Club headquarters to an old brown Army tent in the Vinciguerras' backyard, and begin plotting the day's adventures. We're missing tent poles, but compensate by throwing the canvas over an unused section of clothesline. We all think we're pretty cool hanging out in the tent, even though it's hotter than hell inside with the sun beating down.

David steals a pack of his Dad's cigarettes and a book of matches. He says there's enough for everybody to give it a try. He's a somewhat experienced smoker for his age, or so he lets on. I'm not too excited about the idea, but the way that he's putting on airs, I'm bound to follow along. Bobby, Pauly, Leo, Joey, and I pile into the tent behind David. He hands out cigarettes. He thinks he's the Marlboro man, instructing us how to hold the cigarettes, light them, and tip the ashes. He even tries to demonstrate how to blow a smoke ring. We're all watching him, but he's interrupted by a high-pitched voice from the back of the tent. It's Little Pauly.

Light me up!

There's a fresh butt hanging from his lips, and Pauly's anxious to get started. He's a born competitor, determined to blow the best smoke rings in the tent. He's the runt of our gang, with three older brothers. This

compels him to try harder than all the rest of us at everything. His acquired taste for charcoal seems to make
cigarettes the logical next step.

Halfway through my first smoke I need remedial
training from David on the breathing part. The tent's
spinning. I feel a strong desire to puke. Two doors away,
my mom's hanging laundry on our clothesline and notices smoke billowing out of the tent. She watches me
exit in great distress and throw myself on the lawn,
choking in agony.

There's no sympathy from inside the tent. While rolling on the lawn I overhear talk of playing cards the next
time we smoke. Leo chides me.

*Keep it down or you'll get us all in trouble, you big
baby!*

I'm gasping for my life and David's lighting up another smoke inside. Bobby's struggling, too, but he's a
lot more composed than I am. Little Pauly is as cool as
ever. Sometimes I really hate Little Pauly.

After what seems like ages the sky stops spinning
and I'm able to breathe again. I pick myself up off the
lawn and begin the retreat towards home. Mom's looking on, ready to hurl obvious questions into my green
face. I see her facial expression and start to limp.

Were you boys smoking in that tent?

No, Mom, I say, trying to do my best impersonation
of Little Pauly.

Don't lie to me, I can smell it on you!

I play the sympathy card to distract her. *I don't feel
so good, Mom!*

**That's what you get for smoking! I can see
the smoke coming out of that tent, you know!**

Sympathy's nowhere to be found on Kenwick Drive today, so I attempt another diversion.

Oh, I know, Mom, and I told everyone that they shouldn't play with matches.

Who's smoking in that tent, Lugi?

I hesitate to answer, but it's academic after unhappy boys begin to exit amidst loud coughing noises. Each flap of the tent opening releases a fresh cloud of smoke. Leo's standing next to the tent and I feel his unfriendly glare as he watches Mom interrogate me.

It's gonna be a long day.

• • •

In the summer we resolve many disputes with sticks and stones. The battle in progress features a brothers' match, Viscontis versus Vinciguerras. We both have gravel driveways. Errant stones land on the Wrobbels' front lawn. There's three of them against two of us, because despite his age, Little Pauly's a good shot. Nicky emerges and takes our side because he lives next door— but mostly because he knows he'll get hit in the back with rocks if he tries crossing over to enemy lines.

Joey arrives from up the street and provides the Vinciguerras with reinforcement. Like Nicky, he finds this a better choice than getting shot from behind. With the battle raging, Joey comes flying down Kenwick on his bike, a five-speed Schwinn that sounds like a motorcycle from the baseball cards in the wheel spokes. It's the best bike in our club, but Joey doesn't take care of it. That drives everybody nuts on both sides of the rock war. He rarely uses the brakes, opting to jump off while it's still rolling. He doesn't care where it crashes or how hard.

Everyone grabs a branch from nearby willow trees in case there's close-in whip fighting. I make a smoke bomb by filling a sandwich baggie with loose dirt and throw it at Bobby. A mini dust cloud fills the air in front of him. Leo, Nicky, and I fire rocks into the cloud with haste. We don't hear him crying, so everybody must have missed. Both sides wear football helmets and use metal trashcan lids for shields.

Most battles end in a stalemate. A win usually requires that an opponent get hit badly and run into his house, crying and bleeding. Today it's different. Nicky sneaks his way from tree to tree across the street and corners Little Pauly. Shield in one hand and rock in the other he demands unconditional surrender from his much younger and smaller opponent.

Drop it!

Little Pauly, also armed with rock, shield, and helmet, defies him.

No! You drop it!

It's funny to watch, given their difference in age and size. The impasse continues until both sides grow tired of hearing **Drop it!** Peace is declared and warring armies depart the field, but Nicky and Pauly remain to determine which of them has the hardest head. Neither one of them stops issuing threats nor aiming rocks at the other.

I'm warning you Pauly, you better drop it!

No! You drop it!

Mr. Wrobbel emerges from his porch to make both of them drop it. Then he orders all of us to clean up the stones in his front yard.

●●●

The Wrobbels keep their best weapon against us tied up in their backyard—their dog, Tippy. If not the front, at least their backyard is safe from warring juveniles. Tippy's a medium-sized beagle-collie mix. He's the only dog in the neighborhood that's kept tied up. Tippy knows it, too, and this makes him the meanest dog around.

Errant balls that land in the Wrobbels' backyard signal the contest has ended. We like to think we're tough guys... but it's humiliating to knock on their front door to ask for help— especially from a girl.

One day the ball goes into their backyard and I wrongly assume that Tippy's in the house. I don't see him lounging behind a lawn chair. I enter the Wrobbels' backyard to retrieve the ball. As I turn around I see Tippy emerging on the end of a long rope, cutting off my exit. We stand at bay. He doesn't bark or growl or anything. He just stands there on the alert, eyeballing me, daring me to make a move. I cautiously approach and address him in a whimper.

Nice boy, nice Tippy.
Yes, you're a nice boy,
aren't you Tippy?

Now we're face to face. I continue my submissive demeanor. I reach down to pet him, and he becomes the devil incarnate. He takes a good snap at my hand and growls at me with unmistakable hatred.

I bolt from the yard, Tippy hot on my heels. After reaching safety I thank the good Lord for blessing me with the gift of speed. Tippy's incensed by my escape and pulls on his rope in anger, howling with rage.

Whew!

After my close encounter with Tippy, we start calling the Wrobbels' backyard The Wolf Pit.

Another hotly contested game comes to an abrupt end after our ball goes into The Wolf Pit. This time I surrender my pride and knock on the Wrobbels' front door. Diane Wrobbel answers, and right away I know that I'm bothering her. She frowns down at me and remembers every name I ever called her.

Yeah, so what do you want?

She's pissing me off but it's not totally unexpected. I do call her names, but only sometimes and not very often—but sometimes.

We kicked our ball into your backyard.

Yeah, so what?

Well, Tippy's back there.

Yeah, so what? She knows damn well what, and she'll hear some more names as soon as I get my ball back.

Well, I don't want to get bit by Tippy, that's what.

Oh, are you afraid of Tippy? I'll get it for you if you say please!

She's mocking me now, savoring my anxiety. She grins with delight while she closes the door in my face. I've never seen her so happy in my life and retreat to the sound of fading laughter.

She never does get us the ball, either. I make a mental note to devise a new name for her.

• • •

I live in world where most parents employ corporal punishment. The few that don't face open disparagement from their peers. If So-and-So's kid's a brat, it's because his parents don't believe in spanking him. It's the motivational tool of choice among parents, teachers, coaches, peers, and playground bullies alike—and it's quite effective, from where I'm standing.

In our household, Mom fills the role of Beatings Administrator. She performs her duties with gusto whenever the situation calls for it, and at other times just to be safe. Dad never spanks us—he can freeze us in our tracks with a look—so we save our worst behavior for the times he's not around.

God forbid if anyone dares to accuse the Visconti parents of not spanking their kids. I try to make them look good to their friends and interrupt a social visit to display the spanking paddle.

And this is what our parents hit us with!

I'm smiling and holding up the working end of a wooden paddle-and-rubber-ball toy, minus rubber ball, rubber band, and the staples that hold them together.

I think I'm doing them a favor. Now everybody knows they're not among the bad parents who don't spank their kids. Mom looks embarrassed while Dad's

The Hairy Eyeball

giving me the hairy eyeball. I just scheduled an appointment with the paddle after the guests depart.

It doesn't matter if I hide the paddle because there's always a wooden spoon handy. If not, Mom's great skills of improvisation always provide alternatives. I'm standing in the kitchen with her. She's armed with a spoon and I'm foolish enough to attempt defiance. The spoon comes down and I instinctively lift an arm to deflect the incoming utensil-turned-weapon. After colliding with the bony part of my elbow it snaps in two pieces, and I don't feel a thing! Mom's left holding the spoon shaft, or the short end of the stick, as it were. Together we watch the round part spin on the floor until it stops, both of us too surprised to speak. After the silence ends I'm accused of breaking her spoon and flee in haste, knowing of her ability to improvise.

Soon afterward, a similar situation unfolds in our auxiliary kitchen in the cellar. I suspect that Italian mothers around the world have extra kitchens just to keep wooden spoons handy. Another act of defiance produces similar results. The spoon approaches but this time I'm standing a little further away. Instead of putting my elbow out—a proven defensive move—I extend my arm, hand, and fingers straight out and tense the muscles in anticipation of contact with the incoming utensil. The wooden spoon connects with tensed fingertips and splits in half, the long way. We're both shocked, but I'm in ecstasy. I *Kung Fu'd* the spoon. It's the coolest thing that I've ever done in my life.

Final Score:

Lugi - 2
Spoons - Nada

• • •

I should have stuck with the spoons. My Brother
Leo's size and my temper make life painfully inconven-
ient for me sometimes. I barely make it up to his
shoulders in height and also come up short in relative
poundage and strength. There's many one-sided beatings that end with me absorbing blows until Leo decides
I've had enough, or I'm saved by Mom—whichever
comes first.

Mom, Terry, Leo, and I sit around the small table in
our kitchen having lunch. I'm arguing with Leo. He in-
cites me to a rage. I throw a meatball, with sauce, across
the table directly into his face. I'm seeing red—I have to
do *something* to stop his lips from moving.

It does.

I later wish that he kept talking. Instead he gets up,
pulls me out of my chair, and delivers a series of body
blows that make the Kenwick Hall of Fame. He's a fast
puncher, too, and it ends before Mom can intervene. She
steps over my prostrate body on the floor and gives Leo
a smack or two, *just because*. I avoid him for days afterward and swear vengeance. But I keep all future
meatballs on my plate.

The only thing more dangerous than having a
brother who's two years older is having a sister who's
four years older. I do my best to live up to her proclama-
tion.

You're a brat, and you've always been a brat!

I torment my sister whenever the opportunity presents itself, and at various other moments of great
inspiration. It's an uneventful day, so I comment that

her breath smells like corn husks. I don't know where this revelation came from, but I'm on an anti-vegetable kick. I follow it up with a remark that the backs of her legs look like artichokes.

Whether from Catholic mysticism or Italian superstition, obsessions run in our family. Terry's infatuated with the number three, often expressed in her famous warning.

You better knock it off or I'll give you three good ones!

In her three-part lessons it doesn't matter if the first one she lands is a good one. That only means that you're unlucky—two more are on their way. I learn alternative meanings to the *three strikes and you're out* rule.

At the end of a high-intensity episode of *three strikes*, Terry surprises me. I think it's over after getting bashed for the third time, but wrongly assume that she's gained satisfaction. Far from it. She feints walking away, turns suddenly and grabs me by the closest body parts available. I'm thrown into the far corner of the room. Before I know what's happening I see her bearing down on me. She's gaining speed, bad intentions plainly visible on her face, and never breaks stride. At the end of her run she turns her body around and plants her nether region into my midsection, effectively driving my carcass into the wall while removing the air from my lungs.

I collapse in a heap, gasping for breath, incapable of crying out for help. Mom's nowhere in sight. Reminiscent of Pearl Harbor, I'm lucky she doesn't come back to finish me off. It's my belief that word of her technique reaches the professional wrestling circuit—and becomes known as throwing your opponent into the turnbuckle.

•••

CHAPTER NINE

TRAJECTORIES

Bobby learns how to ride a two-wheeler before me, and it's a panic situation. I should have learned first because I'm older. Now it's just me and Little Pauly on three or more wheels.

There's no way that Pauly's going to learn how to ride a bike before I do.

The next day I endure public ridicule during repeated attempts to master two-wheeled balance. Terry's bike is too big for me—still it's nice of her to let me use it. Leo's bike fits me better, but he says I'll ruin it and Mom's not making him cooperate. I don't recall defying her lately, but there it is.

The self-taught lessons follow an observable pattern.

    a) Walk bike uphill to top of street.
    b) Point bike downhill.
    c) Carefully climb on.
    d) Apply law of gravity.
    e) Coast downhill and alternatively touch feet to ground to remain upright.
    f) Jump off bike into bush at bottom of hill.

g) Ensure prior step completed before reaching intersection.
h) Extract self from bush, retrieve bike, try again.

Each training run down Kenwick Drive ends with me in the bushes, with or without the bike. I can't figure out how to reach the pedal brake and keep my balance at the same time. The bushes help soften my fall. Plus I'd rather get scratched by shrubbery than break a bone on the sidewalk. It's amazing how far the bike can travel upright without me on it. I watch in extreme frustration while enduring multiple scrapes and scratches. Extracting myself from the bushes once again, I run to retrieve the bike for another attempt. The Kenwick boys howl ridicule at me.

The number of spectators gradually increases. Half the neighbors watch from the street and the other half looks out of their windows. Some encourage me, others cheer for the bush, and a third faction roots for the bike. The boys jeer as I go past my house, by this time having gained enough speed to make Fred Astaire proud of my toe tapping with both feet.

My confidence starts to wane from the mockery when I spot Little Pauly heading toward one of his brothers' bikes. It looks like he's getting ideas. A vision of Pauly riding a bike and smiling overwhelms me. I snatch Terry's bike off the sidewalk for another try.

A happy accident occurs.

With Pauly Panic raging, I drive *across* the street instead of downhill. I find myself riding on two wheels with my feet on the pedals, no tap dancing required.

This is easy!

I'm in heaven, but the euphoria doesn't last long.

Having mastered the art of balance, I next learn about the pedal brakes on Terry's bike. Sometimes they work and sometimes they don't. I'm riding in blissful oblivion and encounter one car coming toward me and another parked in my immediate path. I peddle backward, expecting to slow down.

The brakes don't work.

Somewhere I missed a lesson or two in Driver Ed.

The way I see it there are two choices—hit the moving car or hit the parked car. I select the parked car. Somehow I overlook a third option to jump off the moving bike, despite having mastered the skill. I attribute this to the absence of a bush at the crash site.

Brakeless bike and rider crash into the front bumper of the parked vehicle. I slide along the pavement under the car, the bike wedged in between us. The inside of my left thigh gets caught in the chain or the spokes of a wheel, or both, and a decent sized chunk of flesh gets torn out of my leg. Luckily I don't know it yet. I'm in a daze under the car, and see an upside-down vision of kids running to my aid, having witnessed the catastrophe.

God works in mysterious ways. First He allows me to put on a show for the neighborhood, then He transforms the audience into first responders during the grand finale.

My rescuers remove the bike and help me get out from under the car. They observe the ugly wound visible on my limb, but I'm the last to know that I have a hole in my leg. Some kids point, others wince, and although the emotional shock saves me from pain I instinctively start to cry. Terry's gawking at the mess on my leg and loses her nerve. She supports me in the best way that she can and starts to yell.

Run home! Run home! Run home!

I take her advice and throw in a few screams along the way. Upon arrival I'm packed into the family car and hurried to the nearby doctor's office for tetanus shots and stitches. Dad pinches the hole in my leg closed while the Doctor sews it shut and reassures me.

You're a brave boy!

Dad tells me to squeeze his hand and not to look while the Doctor stitches.

• • •

While I'm sidelined with stitches in my leg I experience yet another episode of God working in mysterious ways.

Mom and Dad buy me a new bike.

They don't want me to be afraid to ride a bike again, so they enact the old saying about getting back on the horse after you fall off.

I'm ordered to restrict my activities until the stiches come out. Of course I willingly comply. I'm watching TV, and a commercial comes on encouraging kids to hold a fundraising carnival to benefit the Muscular Dystrophy Association. The pitch strikes a chord with me because I'm wounded, so I raise the issue at the next meeting of the Science Club. And it sounds fun, with or without the bandaged leg.

At the meeting everyone agrees that it's a good idea. We get the details and send away for the how-to kit that comes in the mail. We're all excited for the kit to arrive, but we commence planning our first carnival without it. Everybody wants the carnival to be held in their own yard, and a lively debate ensues. Threats of rival carnivals dampen the festive mood. It's a relief to hear the others consent that club headquarters is the best location.

In addition to his Presidential duties, Nicky's our club's resident handyman—so he takes the lead in most of the construction work. He supervises everything else, too. He's really getting on my nerves.

Our carnival boasts a variety of attractions for potential customers, with many opportunities for us to separate them from their pennies, nickels, and dimes. Nicky creates a rollercoaster rig of sorts, and we're counting on it to become the top moneymaker. The backyard garage, destined never to see a car, becomes transformed into a haunted house. It's already kind of creepy in daylight, but with the overhead door closed and towels covering the two small windows it's downright scary. We'll bring the customers into the garage through our cellar. Once inside, they can put their hands in jars of various gooey substances purported to be human guts. We hang Halloween masks and decorations on the walls. Leo tells me to shut up after I tell him that nobody can see the decorations because it's too dark in there. Joey says he'll hide behind the door under a sheet and jump out screaming to startle the customers.

We plan a variety of games like ring toss, bucket ball, knocking down plastic bowling pins with a whiffle ball, and throwing bean bags into holes cut out of a sheet of plywood. I like the bean bag game because Nicky lets me paint the plywood. Bobby says we're going to be rich.

Our concession table features a choice of Kool-Aid or lemonade, and several Moms volunteer to provide cookies and brownies, too. Nicky's little sister Susie gets assigned to work the concession table because she's a girl, and we certainly can't tell our older sisters what to do.

We don't look down on Susie, though. In fact, somebody gets the idea to make her a stove out of used tricycle parts. I understand how the handle bar might work for a gas line (if it's hollow), but I can't figure out how we'll make the rest of the stove from the other parts.

There's an easy answer. Nicky says he can do it, and I'm told to shut up again.

Carnival construction proceeds at a good pace with anticipation growing for the big event. After the stiches come out I ride my new bike throughout the neighborhood to post advertisements on telephone poles and trees. Bonus: Little Pauly's still on his trike, freaked out after what happened to me.

Nicky says that he'll tell the kids in Lyncourt School. We expect a good turnout for carnival day.

The following afternoon the club's together and Nicky comes running into our backyard.

Hey guys! I heard at school there's a pond full of pollywogs in Lyncourt! I know where it is—we can get there on our bikes. And we can sell pollywogs at the carnival!

We gather buckets, plastic bowls, and an assortment of fish tank and butterfly nets. Riding our stingray bikes, we set off on the next adventure. It's a long journey—an entire mile—to the other side of Lyncourt. As long as we're back in time for dinner there's no harm done. We feel it's considerate of us not to trouble our Moms with asking for permission first.

The pond's right where Nicky said it was, behind Henry's Hamburgers on New Court Road. It's really more of a supersized puddle than a pond, an accumulation of runoff from the neighborhood after heavy rains. It's filled with dark, brackish water and it's located in a swampy area, so I guess that makes it a pond. Upon arrival there's already a bunch of kids fishing for pollywogs.

They eye us with suspicion. I anticipate trouble because we're on their turf, but Nicky's on our side so we're safe.

Our leader breaks the ice and engages them in friendly conversation. The tension clears. They're actually nice kids, eager to tell us how many they caught. The pond's chock full of pollywogs—there's more than enough for everyone. We're shown the best techniques to use and, following the kids' expert advice, we soon accumulate a good haul for the return trip home.

The pond's only a few feet deep and I could throw a stone across it without much difficulty. Still, it's big enough to contain a mini-island in the middle. An unknown girl wades to the island. She slips, falls in, and screams. This is enough for Nicky, a born hero with a flair for the dramatic, to spring into action.

Slogging twenty feet through shallow water would allow him to reach her quickly, but that's not fast enough. Instead, he performs a Tarzan dive from shore and attempts to swim to her. The pond's too shallow for swimming and his impressive overhead strokes in the murky water get him nowhere fast. The violent splashing gets the girl's attention and she stands up to watch, effectively spoiling the dramatic rescue. Not to be thwarted, our hero finally arrives and swoops the maiden into his arms to carry her safely to shore. All of the kids at the pond watch the spectacle. More than a few of us want to see him slip and dump the pair of them back into the pond. Nicky's soaked and says he wants to depart with our buckets of pollywogs.

It's a miserable ride back home.

Getting there with empty containers is one thing, riding home carrying puddle water and pollywogs is another. Our inventory suffers along the way, but there's still plenty left for the pollywog booth at the Fair.

●●●

The big day arrives! It's agreed that we'll sell polly-wogs for a penny apiece. We make a sign announcing the amazing deal, while Mom provides sandwich baggies for transportation. To entice a fifty pollywog minimum, we offer an empty Cool Whip container and lid for no extra cost. Pollywog sales are brisk, and now we're getting two cents for the ones with little legs.

We hoped to draw a crowd, but now that it's happening, we're kind of surprised. There's a line for the rollercoaster, and the haunted house gets rave reviews. The bigger kids enjoy the fright from Joey jumping out and screaming, but after a little kid cries nobody smaller than Little Pauly is allowed in. Susie is busy selling refreshments. We forget that she can't count. Although most of the product is gone, there's not many coins in the till. That, and she got a late start collecting—nobody told her that she's supposed to sell stuff, not give it away.

The carnival comes to an abrupt halt when a customer announces that he wants to buy five dollars' worth of pollywogs. An unheard-of amount. Everyone's in shock, customers and carnies alike. The young customer's a stranger to our neighborhood, but he's standing there with a five dollar bill in his hand, determined to do business.

Nicky grabs an old bucket from his garage. Due to the size of the transaction he says he'll handle it personally. Using a small fish tank net, he begins to scoop and count five hundred pollywogs, making the transfer from one bucket to another and not forgetting to count off two for the ones with little legs.

One, two, three, he begins.

Forty-seven, forty-eight, forty-nine, he continues after a while.

Three-hundred and twelve, Three-hundred and thirteen, he says after an eternity.

Four-hundred ninety eight, four-hundred ninety nine, FIVE HUNDRED!

It's starting to get dark and the stranger is the only person left besides the carnies. Our customer's thrilled to walk away with a bucket of five hundred pollywogs and we all stare in amazement at a real five-dollar bill.

There's big plans for our windfall. We envision ourselves making trunkloads more. I like the idea of taking the show on the road with my new bike. If the next show's beyond peddling distance I'll have the conductor put it on the train for me. We'll need to hire workers, and everyone will be well fed with delicious meals Susie cooks for us on her stove that we made from tricycle parts.

The first cloud to cast a shadow on our vision of utopia soon appears in the form of an unhappy looking man, carrying a familiar looking bucket. He says the five dollars didn't belong to his boy, and he wants his money back, *right now.* Nicky bravely attempts the *all sales are final* line, but the man's demeanor convinces him that the customer is always right. Nicky concedes—but the return transaction process must be accurate and complete.

He retrieves the small fish tank net and begins to scoop and count five hundred pollywogs, not forgetting to count off two for the ones with little legs.

One, two, three, he begins, and the man's face turns red.

Sixteen, seventeen, eighteen, he continues. The man's fuming.

Twenty-seven, twenty-eight, twenty-nine...

And it's over.

The man snatches the five-dollar bill and storms down our driveway, taking our dreams with him. There's dead silence in our backyard. I feel an ache in my gut. The carnival's still a success—but after all the stress, trauma, and paying the staff, we don't have any extra money to send in to the Muscular Dystrophy Association. We remind ourselves that we're scientists, after all—perhaps we could help them in other ways.

• • •

Weeks later we're bored playing backyard carnival games, especially now that nobody's paying. Nicky gets an idea.

Let's go play darts in my basement!

No! It's nice outside—I don't want to play inside, Leo says.

Yeah, Nicky, let's stay outside, David confirms.

Okay, I'll bring the darts outside, he replies, and runs to get them.

A moment later he's back with the darts, but not the board. It's a masterstroke that allows our imaginations to run wild. We get warmed up hitting the street light pole and progress to stalking insects. Nobody's coming close to hitting anything, and hunting bugs gets old pretty fast.

We soon return to the competitive nature of darts, and our strong desires to win. Contests of *Who can throw the highest?* and *Who can throw the farthest?* commence on Kenwick Drive. I find *Who can throw the highest?* very disconcerting. If anyone's going to catch one in the head, it's me.

David gets an idea for a new game.

*Let's see who can throw one the highest **and** the farthest!*

With that he throws a dart upward with all his might. The dart climbs higher and higher as we all watch in amazement. The downward trajectory takes aim at the station wagon parked in the Savastanos' driveway. Amazement becomes horror, especially for David.

Time slows to a crawl. The dart takes forever to find the rectangular back window of the station wagon. After a second or two of utter silence the window cracks, a hundred jagged lines running outward from the dart's tip. A second more and the glass shatters into the back seat and all over the driveway.

It's an eerie sound. The neighbors pick up on it quickly, including Mr. Savastano. Windows and doors start opening on Kenwick Drive and we all turn pale. I didn't know David could run that fast. The rest of us remain frozen, all wearing the famous deer-in-the-headlights look.

Nobody knows what's to become of David, but I'm guessing that his Dad picks up the tab for Mr. Savastano's window along with his belt for David's behind. For Nicky it's more cut and dried. Upon seeing him with a dart in his hand and another in the driveway, Mr. Savastano quickly dispenses justice. Nicky's exaggerated screams fill the neighborhood while he's unceremoniously ushered back inside. I hear muffled admonishments from inside the house. We all scatter.

From a safe distance we watch angry Mr. Savastano and crying Nicky clean up the glass from the driveway and the inside of the station wagon. And of course they're wearing gloves. It's dangerous otherwise—kind of like throwing darts outside.

• • •

On hot summer nights the upstairs of our house feels like a furnace. It's the last week of summer vacation, and Mom says it's okay if we want to sleep on our front porch. She even lets us stay up late to watch *The Tonight Show* on TV. Dad enclosed the porch with storm windows soon after we moved in—after we nearly killed ourselves jumping from its unenclosed knee walls. It's large enough to fit an old couch, a chaise lounge, and a rocking chair. We inhabit our porch during three seasons—in the winter, it becomes a walk-in freezer.

There's three of us on the porch—Terry, Leo, and me—after Mom set up an old cot for the third person to use. We're told to get to sleep after she turns off the TV in the adjacent living room, and goes to bed herself. Dad retired earlier. We're starting to doze when I hear a sound coming from next door. I sit up a little and turn my head to see Mr. Wrobbel emerge from his front door. He plants himself on his top step, quietly observing the neighborhood and taking in the air. I dismiss any concern and settle back down to sleep.

Hearing more movement, I sit up again to see what he's up to now. As it turns out, not much. He's slowly pacing back and forth in front of his house, not really doing anything. Once again I settle back down to sleep.

Everything's quiet.

Then I'm startled to hear footsteps on *our* front stairs. It's Mr. Wrobbel again, and now, after climbing up our five stairs, he's standing right at our front door! Through my half-closed eyelids I watch him bend over and peer inside our porch. I hold my breath, afraid to move a muscle. I wonder if he's going to ring the doorbell.

Then he stands upright and turns back toward the street, surveying the neighborhood. Maybe he just wants to see what the street looks like from our front door in the middle of the night. I don't know—this *is* Kenwick Drive.

And then he cuts one!

No mistake about it, Mr. Wrobbel's standing on our front steps in the middle of the night cutting farts. My mind starts racing. Is *that* what he's up to? Does he do this often? How many nights have I slept peacefully upstairs with Mr. Wrobbel farting on our front stairs?

It remains one of life's deepest unsolved mysteries.

•••

CHAPTER TEN

THE REEL-TO-REEL

I'm in third grade and no longer believe in Santa, but I miss looking for burn marks in the back of the fireplace. Instead, in the weeks before Christmas I enjoy the thrill of searching the house for unwrapped presents, a pastime that's quite enjoyable until you get caught. Leo and I find a Hot Wheels racetrack in Mom's closet. It draws us like moths to a flame. We're deep inside the closet, mesmerized by Hot Wheels, and don't hear her approaching until she's right behind us.

Well, I guess I don't have to bother wrapping any-thing this year, she says sadly.

We feel bad for her and plead.

No! Wait, Mom! Please wrap the presents—we'll stay out of the closet from now on!

Surprisingly, she does, but we don't keep our end of the bargain. We continue to look for other hiding places. She tries to use the attic for concealment and I counter by having Leo go in first. There we find the cars that go with the track. Yay!

Christmas morning arrives. We try to act surprised by the non-clothing presents under the tree. I'm consumed with Hot Wheels and don't miss Santa at all.

Later that winter we're getting cabin fever. I decide to try ice skating on Kenwick Drive. It's a spontaneous act to relieve boredom during a snowstorm. It happens at night, so I'm wearing my pajamas. There's nothing good on TV, so with Mom and Dad safely out of the way in the kitchen, I make my move. Without a word I snatch my sister's white ice skates from the closet and put them on while Leo and Terry gawk. I throw on a winter coat over my PJs and a long stocking cap with a ball on the end—the kind that doubles as a hat and scarf. The hat goes well with PJs if you skate in the street at night during a snowstorm. I'm out the front door before anyone can stop me.

It's hard to get down the front steps with the skates on. I never thought of that. Leo and Terry watch at the door in disbelief while I slog my way out to the street. It's cold on my PJ-clad legs, but I've come too far not to skate. Just like during the neighborhood kickball games in the summer, I'm amazed by how many motorists are drawn to our normally quiet street. The snowbanks make it dangerous for skaters, too. I'm compelled to dive into one whenever a car goes by. Terry later tells me that after each dive she could see only my PJ bottoms and her white skates sticking out of the drifts.

The skating is hard going, but I'm having a blast. Neighbors start peering out their windows to observe the spectacle. They must be bored, too, Or maybe it's just fun to watch a kid in PJs and a long stocking cap skating in the road at night during a blizzard.

Not a person to play second fiddle to his younger brother, Leo darts outside wearing only his PJs. I'm surprised because we only have one pair of skates, but his intentions soon become clear. I'm thrown into the snowbank and he runs back inside. He's crazier than I am because he's only wearing slippers on his feet. I pull myself from the snowbank, but his prank gets a lot of snow down my back and now I need more than just PJs under my coat. Mom yells for me to come in. For once I listen to her.

• • •

The roof of the front porch is right outside our bedroom window—perfect for making snowballs whenever we need one. It's great—we can ambush Terry in the hallway when she's not expecting it, or make a bunch and have a snowball fight inside the house. That's all fun, but it means getting in trouble after Terry opens her big mouth or Mom finds puddles on the floor from old snowballs.

We like bombing houses better. We make snowballs in our bedroom and wing sidearm shots at the Wrobbels' house next door. It's an activity best enjoyed at night. The impact of snowballs against the glass storm windows makes a loud, satisfying noise. We peek out our bedroom window to watch what happens. Various occupants enter the porch searching for clues and suspicious looking persons outside. They retire empty-handed but soon reappear after another round of snowballs blast against their porch windows. It's too much fun, and somehow we manage not to overdo it. We wait a few days to repeat the caper.

The next time I lean too far out the bedroom window to get a better look at the chaos, and they spot me. I see lips moving and fingers pointing. It's easy to guess what's being said. Within seconds the phone rings, and Mom and Dad hear it from our unhappy neighbors. They're in our room a moment later for the interrogation, with Dad playing the lead investigator.

Why did you do it?

My knee-jerk reaction is to tell the truth and say *because their house is within range,* but I provide the standard response.

I don't know.

Don't tell me that! Why did you do it?

The second truthful response is to say *because we could,* but this feels even worse and I stick to my guns.

I don't know.

Well, I'll give you two weeks to think about it—how's that? Now you're grounded!

We've heard this before. Dad only hands out two-week sentences—no more, no less. On occasion, and only when he's safely beyond earshot, I've been known to mimic his judicial pronouncements. Leo tells me that I do his voice pretty good.

Less than a week into the grounding we're having stealth withdrawal, and turn our sights to the Savastanos' house on the other side. We silently open the front window, make two snowballs, and open the side window facing our next victim. It's nighttime and easy for us to see Mr. Savastano sitting at his kitchen table.

After the first snowball hits, he reacts with swift precision—as if he's been practicing what to do in case his house got hit by a snowball at night. With equal determination and efficiency he rises from the table and flicks off the kitchen light, enabling him to see outside. One glance shows him the open window in our bedroom and seconds later the phone rings. We get it worse this time, with additional grounding discussed in terms of birthdays.

Undeterred, we next turn our sights to moving targets, those being passing motorists. This feat requires a strong arm, great timing, and a bit of luck—all of which I lack, so it's up to Leo. I contribute by spotting cars, watching for nosy neighbors, and making snowballs for him. He pulls off the miracle shot, nailing one after many unsuccessful attempts, all from the safety and comfort of our own bedroom. The car comes to an abrupt halt. We're delighted when an angry driver emerges, hoping to get his hands on the nearest guilty-looking kid.

•••

Having one bathroom for five people often leads to problems, particularly if everybody's home and you need to go pee in the morning. In times of crisis I often resort to using our backyard, which provides several spots of relative privacy for boys who can't hold it anymore. During the winter, though, the deep snow buries all of the best peeing spots. It's a winter morning and I'm waiting on the stairs outside the bathroom for my turn while Dad takes a shower. I hear all of his loud shower noises—you know the kind? I don't know why hot running water makes people utter loud *Ahhs* and *Ohhs*. Dad's gifted with this talent. Today it amplifies my agony. I mimic him from the stairs, holding pee up to my eyeballs.

After reaching the breaking point, I grab ahold of myself and waddle to the back door. I start doing the pee dance on the inside stoop. There's no stopping nature. I direct a violent stream into the snow from the back door. I'm relieved in two ways, the second being that none of our backyard neighbors happen to see me in my glory.

Later that morning, however, Mom goes to throw stale bread outside for the birds. She opens the back door, sees the yellow snow, and starts asking questions.

Lugi, did you go pee out the back door?

No.

Don't lie to me – I saw that yellow snow!

It must have been a dog.

But there's no footprints! Should I ask your brother?

Uhhh...

That pretty much ends the conversation. There's no comeback for her forensics. I curse the birds and the stale bread. Learning from my mistake, I change tactics, safe in the knowledge that Mom never throws stale bread on the front porch roof. It's riskier, though, going pee out of my bedroom window in the front of the house. It requires constant head turning to look for neighbors. Sometimes this makes you miss the roof, but so far I haven't had to explain what I need those paper towels for. I'll have to ask Leo for a good excuse.

• • •

The classrooms at Assumption Catholic are heated by radiators along the wall, which we sometimes use to dry our wet hats and gloves after coming in from the snow. We'd sit on them if we could, but if you sat there too long you'd burn your bottom. The radiators clink and clank. Every once in a while they abruptly throw a loud, startling sound that makes me wonder if one of them is about to explode.

It's a winter day during recess and I find myself alone in our classroom with John, a boy of questionable repute. Our teacher is down the hall supervising our classmates waiting in line to use the boys' and girls' lavatories. John gets an idea.

Hey Louie, let's pee on the radiator and see what happens.

Why?

I just told you, idiot, to see what happens.

John used to be in my brother's class, but he got held back a year. Because he's older and has a reputation for trouble, most of us try hard to impress him.

Okay, I reply, and he runs to the door to make sure nobody's coming. It's a strange feeling, standing there in the empty classroom with John, both our dinks out, peeing on the radiator. The hot radiator hisses in protest after catching the spray, and in no time the liquid begins to evaporate toward the ceiling. We name it The Pee Fog.

Neither one of us expected that the Pee Fog would stink. Old radiators and pee don't mix, though, and Sister's nose detects an odor. She sniffs around the room to detect the source and sees a trace of partly evaporated something-or-other on the radiator. She quickly makes a connection between the smell and John of questionable repute, recently left unsupervised in her classroom. She turns to me for an explanation.

Louis, did you or John put something on the radiator?

No, Sister.

Hmmm.

The three of us stand in front of the radiator and John observes the evidence fading away while it dries. He braves a question.

Uh, Sister, why do you think we put something on the radiator? It's awful old, you know.

Don't get smart with me Mister! I can see there's something on the radiator!

See what, Sister?

The stain on the radiator! And lying about it will only make it worse for you!

What stain?

I stand in silence watching the exchange, unaware of this tactical intelligence. Sister points an angry finger at the now invisible trace of our crime, and catches herself about to say something. John repeats the question in a meek and innocent tone.

What stain, Sister?

She stands in wary stillness for a moment, then suddenly gives up and tells us to stay out of trouble while she calls for the janitor. John casts a mischievous smile at me while she departs. We're both greatly admired by the other boys after we tell them what happened. The kids who sit closest to the radiator have other feelings, but they keep them to themselves.

•••

There's lots of nearby sledding options for us in the winter. Even though we bombed the Wrobbels' porch windows with snowballs, they still let us play on the short, steep hill in their backyard. Everybody on the block wants to sled there because it's so close, but every run ends with a crash into a fence, tree, or bush. I like the hill at Webster School the best. It's fantastic when it's icy. It draws kids from miles around. The only drawbacks are waiting in line for a turn or picking up so much speed that you can't stop until you're in the road. Sledding on the hill in front of our house isn't bad after a fresh snow, but the hill on Rivoli Avenue, right around the corner, is steeper and faster, especially when there's an icy glaze on the road.

Today's an icy day on Rivoli. Leo's riding our wooden sled with twin metal runners. He gains excellent speed, and approaches the intersection with Pleasantview Ave., where there's no stop sign. A car's coming! To avoid a collision he steers toward a snowbank, but it's sloped and suddenly he's airborne—with him traveling in one direction and the sled in another. The sled lands unharmed on a snow-covered lawn, but Leo does a bellysmacker on the road. Onlookers groan after he lands. He curls up in a ball, holding onto the family jewels.

As he's lying there in agony we load him aboard his sled, more useful now as a stretcher. Two of us grab the clothesline attached to the front and pull him back up the hill, running all the way. At the top of Rivoli and Kenwick I want to ride him back home. I envision the neighbors cheering the greatest act of chivalry and valor ever witnessed on Kenwick Drive. Instead I'm denied my opportunity to play the hero—Leo recovers and pushes me off.

• • •

Mom keeps getting bigger and bigger this winter, and by spring she's huge. Early one April morning Dad takes her to St. Mary's Hospital on Court Street to have a baby. My great-aunt Mary Gilbert comes over to watch us. This is a first. She's as old as Gramma. When Aunt Mary's not around, Gramma says she puts too much bread in her meatballs.

Doze not a meatballs, doze a breadballs.

Aunt Mary wants to know if we ate breakfast. We tell her we're out of eggs and cereal. She spots an almost empty bag of sliced bread on the counter. I tell her that we don't eat the end slices but she says it's still good. Into the toaster it goes. She spreads peanut butter and jelly on it and soon I'm eating the end piece of toast.

What do you know? Aunt Mary was right— the end pieces aren't so bad. I start to ask her if she uses them in her breadballs, but Leo cuts me off.

The next day a much slimmer Mom comes home carrying my little sister Maria. Right away we start calling her Mimi. The spare room is now Mimi's room. Why do the girls always get to have their own rooms... even babies?

•••

We love to play with the small reel-to-reel tape recorder, but we can only use it with Leo's permission and under his supervision. Terry and I get to handle it, but technically it belongs to Leo because he got it for his birthday. Mom is sometimes frugal with birthday presents, and has been known to qualify them with a saying that the recipient hates to hear.

It's yours, but it's for all of you...

Leo doesn't follow the letter of the law concerning the *all of you* part. Terry and I find it safer to ask him first whenever we want to use it.

We're pretty creative with the recordings we make— it's a great diversion whenever we're stuck inside. We pretend we're doing a radio show, and read out the story in a comic book. It's the most fun if our friends join us because there's more opportunities for bloopers. The cast of characters gets divvied up, and everybody gets a turn to read whenever their character speaks in the story. Terry's the oldest, so she usually gets to be the narrator in addition to other female characters. We all contribute sound effects. The scary comics always produce the best bloopers because we're trying hard to be serious and it's impossible. We're in the middle of a ghost radio show, and Terry gets a great line.

Peeuuww!! The smell of sulphur chokes me!

Besides reading comics, we make up our own characters and scenarios. Leo and I create Horace Borden, a starving homosexual played by Leo, and a nameless old grouch, played by me. The old grouch becomes the unfortunate target of Horace's desires for food and sex. The scene opens with sound of wind blowing, and the old man snoring, farting, and groaning inside his house. Horace knocks at his door. We don't bother to explain how or why Horace would be knocking on the old man's door, it just happens. The sound effects include door knocking and the old man's waking sounds—grunting and mumbling—footsteps, and finally a door opening. I improvise a crotchety old voice.

Yeah? What do you want?

Leo, in the role of Horace, answers in a nerdy, effeminate tone.

Hello, my name is Horace Borden, can I come in?

Horace doesn't wait for permission and enters.

NO! Hey, get out of here! What are you doing?

Punching noises follow these protests.

Please, just let me stay for a little while—it's cold outside!

More wind noises.

All right, but just for a little while.

This only serves to embolden Horace.

Whatcha got to eat? I'm starving!

Again, Horace doesn't wait for an answer, but helps himself.

Hey! Get out of there! Why, you little...!

More punching sounds. Horace groans.

I'm sorry, but I haven't eaten anything for days!

Too bad!

Horace next attempts to appease his other hunger.

You know, I think you're kind of cute! Do you like men?

What?! Hey! Let go of me! What's wrong with you??!

More punching noises. Horace utters,

Oh God, just a little bit!

The skit ends there. The series is dropped during production of Episode Two, which begins with the same opening noises and Horace knocking on the door announcing,

Open Up! It's Horace!

This time Mom's listening from the next room. She starts questioning us about the strange characters. The doorbell rings, and we hastily close the studio to go outside and play.

Another unfinished creation is *The Marco Mexico Show*. It's slated to be a variety show, but gets canceled during Episode One. The show begins with an excited Leo introducing Marco Mexico. For this character, he impersonates the announcer on a TV game show we all watch. We get the audience applause from the TV itself.

It's... the Marco Mexico Show!!
(Loud audience applause.)

But he's not here today...
(Even louder audience applause.)

We stop the tape and discuss the next scene, in which Marco Mexico interviews Horace Borden, the famished homosexual. Marco will bring in the old grouch as a surprise guest and another fight breaks out onstage. Mom overhears the rehearsal and won't allow production of such filth in her house. It's not fair that Mom cheats our fans from enjoying a great show—not to mention the loss of millions in advertising revenue.

● ● ●

There's a love-hate relationship between me and the wooden stairs in our house. I love the stairs as an indoor sledding venue. All you need is a decent-sized cardboard box and a sense of adventure. The only risk occurs if you spin around and find yourself going backwards down the stairs. When there isn't a box handy I enjoy descending at high speed on my fanny. Why walk if you can ride? I jump from the top and plant my behind on the third or fourth stair down to attain speeds that rival the cardboard box. I like the pop-pop sound that I make going down—plus it annoys everyone else in the house, making it a twofer.

The hate part comes from falling down the stairs—a routine and painful event. I'm always falling down the stairs. Most incidents occur wearing socks and traveling upward at unsafe speeds. Sounds of rapid footsteps often precede a crash, followed by tumbling noises and groans heard from the dining room floor. It ends with someone laughing, with or without me groaning along.

We're playing in the living room. I ask Leo for permission to get the tape recorder, and he says okay. I start running and make it upstairs on the second attempt. During the return trip, tape recorder in hand and socks on feet, I slip on the top stair and perform somersaults all the way down. I lay dazed at the bottom of the stairs, certain I've sustained multiple fractures from blunt trauma. Leo comes running. I'm overcome by his unusual display of brotherly love. Stepping over my carcass, he quickly shatters this myth.

You jerk! You broke the tape recorder!

He walks away, examining the moving parts of our prized studio equipment, and never looks back. Terry doesn't bother to get up from the couch and Mom tells me to get out of the way so she can vacuum.

•••

CHAPTER ELEVEN

BROTHERLY LOVE

Third grade comes to an end. Mom brings us to Nunzio's barbershop on the North Side for the annual summer buzz cut. It's actually called a Princeton. Nunzio applies the popular liquid hair product, Vitalis, on top to make us look cool. All the Italian men in the neighborhood frequent Nunzio's for a shave, a haircut, or just to hang out and speak in Italian to each other. There's lots of old Ring magazines for his customers to read, and they idolize the two Rockys—Marciano and Graziano— heroes both. Nunzio thinks he's Rocky. If you nod or move while he's cutting your hair he gives you a little smack in the head. He's the world champion of his barbershop. Of course nobody's allowed to swing back at him.

Leo recently acquired a play barbershop kit. He's anxious to try it out on his first customer. The all-plastic kit includes comb, brush, scissors, straight razor, and a small can of shaving cream. The scissors don't cut, but the razor scrapes painfully. I'm convinced to play along, so he gets busy setting up Leo's Barbershop in our bathroom.

I just need a few minutes to set up, he says. *Take a seat on the stairs—it won't be long!*

He closes the door and takes forever to arrange the barbershop. Everything has to be *just right*—his finicky tendencies are progressing with age.

I grow impatient waiting on the stairs outside the barbershop. I'm about to give up when the door swings open and an excited barber yells, **Next!**

I enter his shop of horrors ignorant of what awaits.

The barber pretends to sweep away cut hairs from the chair with a washcloth, and greets me with a smile.

Yes, sir, step right this way, sir!

He wraps a bath towel around my shoulders. The cruelty begins.

We'll just shorten this up a little bit, sir, he says.

He pats my head with one hand while opening, closing, and waving the plastic scissors in the air with the other.

The barber can't make the inoperable scissors cut hair, but he's determined. He tries a twisting motion that pulls my hair and makes me scream. Undeterred, he attempts the maneuver twice more, both times producing more screams and the same failed results. I'm trapped in the chair. The barber looms over me with his body blocking any means of escape. It's like a Vincent Price movie.

Completely nonchalant, he suggests an alternative.

Perhaps you'd like a shave, sir?

I'm glad to try anything other than a continuation of having my hair pulled out by the roots, and readily agree. The barber heats a washcloth to soften up my face for shaving, just like Nunzio does for his customers. But this barber overdoes it. I shriek as he burns my face.

Not to worry, sir, we'll have that face cooled down in no time!

The barber then hurriedly applies cold water from the sink from his cupped hands, drenching my clothes and flooding the barbershop.

Now, that wasn't so bad, was it, sir? asks the barber. *Let's get on to that shave!*

He lathers my face. I'm expecting him to get more shaving cream into my nose, ears, and mouth than he does, so I allow him to proceed. He runs the plastic razor along my cheeks with varying pressure and it soon causes pain. It's obvious that the barber's learning with each stroke. My face cries out in protest. I reach up to intercept the next swipe, but he takes it all in stride with good humor.

There, let's just get you cleaned up, sir!

He soaks the washcloth again, assuring me this time he won't overheat the water. It's the one thing he does right. After removing the remnants of shaving cream from my face he excitedly holds a small, round plastic mirror to my face.

And how does that look, sir?

It looks awful and feels worse. Ugly welts cover my face and there's long red streaks running in different directions. My skin aches terribly after exposure to scalding water and repeated scrapes with plastic.

I'm getting out of here!

I roughly push my way past the barber, but he's not finished.

Wait sir, you forgot your Vitalis!

He snatches a plastic container of liquid hair product and gives the bottle a big squeeze. A streaming jet of Vitalis goes directly into my right eye. I fall to the floor, screaming in agony, and cover my eye with both hands. It feels like it's burning out of its socket—I'm certain he's blinded me.

Mom hears the bloodcurdling screams. She tries to get into the bathroom, but my corpse blocks the door.

What's going on in there?

Nothing, why? calmly replies the barber.

Mom forces her way in and helps me rinse out my burning orb with water. Then she confiscates the instruments of torture and shutters Leo's Barbershop after his first and only customer departs in tears.

• • •

I know it's summer because I hear the melody of the Mr. Softee ice cream truck making its way through the neighborhood. The Mr. Softee jingle plays without end. I suspect the poor driver hears it in his sleep and wakes up screaming. Between the 24/7 torture song and the endless parade of brats, it's a thankless job indeed.

We suspect the driver's woes, making Mr. Softee an easy mark for harassment. We especially enjoy teaming up on the regular driver, who grows to hate us. He's a young guy with a hippie look—long hair and a scraggly beard. One of our common torments is to yell ***Mr. Softee!*** just to make him stop and wait. Hiding and watching after he stops is amusing, but if you're brave enough to stand there in plain sight and not approach the truck it's even better. The best includes feinting an approach to keep him on his toes. If we're really bored, we spread out along the street to see how many times we can get him to stop and not sell anything.

Things escalate to open battle with Mr. Softee. He delights in driving down our street at high speed with no pretense of stopping. He flips us the middle finger salute if he sees us. It's kind of funny, with the Mr. Softee jingle playing in the background.

After he leaves several disappointed girls at curbside, coins in hand, waving and yelling, **Mr. Softee!** they run home to tell. They think we're mean for laughing at them.

But, Mom, he saw me and he just drove right by!

The Moms aren't amused and call in complaints to the home office.

I'm safely in line behind one of the girls to make a legitimate purchase of ice cream. If looks could kill, I'm a dead man walking. Mr. Softee's often pissed on Kenwick Drive, but it sure beats Vietnam.

Hey Lugi, do you know why Dairy Queen can't get pregnant?

I don't know, Leo—why not?

Because she married Mr. Softee!

•••

Summertime on Kenwick Drive means heading up the street to play baseball at Webster School. We play ball in the street, too, but if we manage to get enough of us together it's always preferable to play on grass with a real dirt infield that includes a built-in home plate and regulation backstop fence. Nine players on both sides isn't required—we're good at improvising and modify the rules to fit any situation. If there's only a few of us, we play Home Run Derby to appease our competitive natures.

It's not uncommon for onlookers to join in, especially if they're carrying their own gloves and bats. Most kids eagerly participate in pick-up games—sometimes we're the onlookers invited to play. There's not a parent in sight. We make the rules and resolve any disputes on our own.

Today's contest fields full teams on both sides. A neighborhood tough guy watches from the top of the backstop. He's climbed up to get a better view and yell insults or ridicule us. I don't know this kid's name, but I've seen him before and know his reputation. He's white, but his thick, curly hair resembles an afro. He's muscular, stocky, and a known bully.

But he sucks at playing baseball, and he knows it.

On the rare occasions that he plays, it's always with smaller kids who know the wisdom of keeping their mouths shut. Seeing him play before, I've snickered and mumbled under my breath at him, but always from a safe distance.

The bully's on top of the backstop, full of himself and feeling free to act with impunity. Both teams grow weary of his verbal abuse. The whispers progress with each inning. A subdued objection from a player provides the opening he's been looking for.

Oh yeah? How about if I come down and beat your ass, huh? I'm ready right now, you little shit!

The game comes to halt, with both teams expecting to see the unfortunate player get pounded. The bully recognizes this and relishes his power. It's obvious that his opponent lacks the will to fight and regrets that he misspoke. This only encourages the bully, who extends the challenge to all present.

And I'll fight anybody brave enough to stick up for this pansy-ass! C'mon! Anybody!!

Bad mistake.

An unemotional voice responds from the outfield.

I'll fight you.

Unbeknownst to the bully, Nicky has joined the game-in-progress on the way to his paper route, and blended in without a fuss. The bully responds without knowing who he's talking to.

Okay! Come and take your beating, then!

He starts climbing down from the backstop but doesn't get far. As he descends, Nicky approaches. Recognizing another person with a reputation, the bully halts. Nicky calls him out, his volume and tone increasing with each step.

Why'd you stop? C'mon, I don't have all day!

And he doesn't, either—he's almost late to go pick up his newspapers. This leaves little time to kick this punk's ass, and he has every intention of doing both on time. A much-deflated voice responds from the backstop.

Oh, I didn't know it was you.

He shows a fine command of the language by not saying anything else, and climbs back up to the top. Nicky stands there silently and waits, but nothing happens.

Okay then, he says, and, completely nonchalant, he departs the infield to grab his bags for carrying newspapers. Still within earshot he fires a parting remark.

Just let me know if you ever change your mind!

Nicky shows me that a confident, calm demeanor can defeat a bully. Even though my team loses the game I feel like a winner walking home.

•••

Since we have two decent hills at our disposal, the Kenwick boys decide to build a go-cart. Nicky's a natural carpenter, mechanic, and sometime chemist, so most of the go-cart construction happens at his house. He's more than into it. He claims to have his Dad's permission to use his tools *any time he wants to*—this, despite the occasional sounds of reproach, smacking noises, and screams coming from inside the Savastano house. We all contribute parts, including plywood, nails, screws, hinges, and wheels of various sizes.

We want to build two go-carts so we can race them, but it's obvious we've only got enough parts for one Soapbox Derby Edsel. Applying our own unique law of gravity, we add cinderblocks for extra weight to make it go faster.

The thing weighs a ton—it takes all of us to push it up the hill for a test run. We only lack a test driver. Nobody volunteers—not even Nicky. The honor naturally falls to the bravest one in the club. I'm grateful for a boost to my ego, even when it comes with the feeling of impending doom. I run home to retrieve my green and white Jets football helmet. As soon as I climb in, everyone's anxious to launch me down the hill. I caution them to hang on a minute while I puff out my chest. I pull left and right on the clothesline to test the steering—this makes the wheels grind against the pavement.

With that, several arms and legs propel go-cart and driver down the hill. I'm picking up speed in the death trap as I notice a car appear on the horizon, heading towards me. As the distance shortens between us I start having flashbacks of the day I learned how to ride a bike. And the aftermath. Panic sets in. Once again my mind becomes consumed with the thought of avoiding the moving car at all cost. I can be a world-class one-dimensional thinker when the situation calls for it.

Right before the car and I pass each other, actually at a safe distance apart, I jerk the clothesline hard to one side. This violently flips over the coffin-on-wheels. I'm trapped upside-down beneath a ton of plywood, nails, wagon wheels, cinderblocks, and clothesline. My knees and feet are up over the Jets helmet. I lay there on my back, crying, anticipating the car running me over—which I'm certain will happen any second.

The small crack of daylight between the remains of our contraption and the pavement provides me with an upside-down image of hell. In a daze, through the face mask of my Jets helmet I see disembodied legs running toward me at high speed. I have a vague feeling of *déjà vu*.

The lucky Jets helmet

Miraculously, I've survived with

minor scrapes and bruises. There's a red welt on my face from the chin strap on my helmet. Otherwise I'm unscathed, except for having the shit scared out of me.

And Broadway Joe and the Jets go on to defeat the Baltimore Colts in Super Bowl III.

• • •

After surviving the go-cart fiasco, I decide to focus on the safer pastime of shooting tennis balls into a coffee can. I cut the bottom out of an empty can and nail it to the overhead beam in our cellar. Here even close shots prove difficult to make. I practice a lot more than Leo and usually win when we play P-I-G, or one-on-one. He's not a happy loser, and suggests a few rule changes.

Let's play so there's no fouls and you can do whatever you want to the other person.

Okay, answers the dope.

I take an early lead in the next match, despite increasingly blatant fouls. I near the scoring mark to win the game. The fouls evolve into assaults, and a vicious body blow puts me on the floor. I want to call a halt. He cons me into continuing.

Don't quit, Lugi. I won't hit you that hard anymore, and you agreed to the rules anyway, remember?

Okay, answers the dope again. Leo's really enjoying the game now.

After sinking the next shot, I find myself on the floor again. I protest.

You said you weren't going to hit me that hard!

I'm sorry, I won't do it again, he replies sheepishly.

Okay, answers the dope. Strike three.

The game doesn't proceed for long until once more I'm on the floor seeing red, saucy meatballs. After a brief recovery I scream, ***I'll kill you!*** and fly at him in a rage, winging haymakers in great succession. Again and again my mad rushes end with him laughing and throwing me to the floor,

even madder than before. He's greatly amused until I connect with a couple of decent shots and show no signs of stopping.

After the last trip to the floor, with me yelling ***I'll kill you!*** for the umpteenth time, he warns, *You better stop!*

This goes unheeded. The next charge ends with him delivering the *coup de grace* to my ribs. I'm in a heap on the cold, tiled floor. He snickers and walks away.

You're an idiot, Lugi. That's what you get for accepting those rules—you just paid for being dumb!

I take consolation in having the last word.

At least I won the game!

Thus ends the Kenwick version of tough love.

• • •

I make peace with Leo after our battle, and we resume shenanigans in our room when we're supposed to be in bed for the night. Our bedroom sits right above the living room and Dad's favorite chair. He's sitting there relaxing and doesn't want to hear thumping noises over the top of his head. He utters threats from his chair, but the noise continues.

When we hear his footsteps on the stairs we know that we've pushed our luck too far. We quickly turn off the lights and get in bed. It's usually bad news when Dad pays one of his infrequent visits to our room. Upon arrival, he flicks on the light and orders us to our feet.

All right, if you can't sleep in your beds then you can sleep in the cellar!

Dad has threatened us with these consequences before, and now he's making good on them. We're marched downstairs to the cellar door. Mom looks up from the living room, unsympathetic. He hurries us down into the cellar and tells us that he'd better not hear a sound.

Then he leaves us there in the dark.

For a moment we stand in shock at what just happened. Our fear of Dad, plus the apprehension of being in the dark cellar all night, has our nerves on edge. After our eyes adjust to the dark, we make beds from piles of dirty laundry and settle down on the cold floor in front of the washing machine.

To our surprise, we find our new lodgings much to our liking! Before long we're happy to be down in the cellar alone at night. Too much so, actually. We begin to play and have a good old time. Dad's on his feet again, only this time we hear him overhead instead of coming up the stairs—though of course both times he has the same bad intentions.

What's next? I wonder. *Is our next stop the back-yard, or maybe the trunk of the car?* The cellar light snaps on. Dad's coming but this time he's followed by Mom.

Uh-oh!

Her maternal instincts in high gear, she gets in between Dad and his would-be prey, baring fangs and claws. Momma Bear's dangerous and takes command.

Leo and Lugi, get upstairs and go to bed right now—and if that baby wakes up you'll all regret it!

Her words come out in a hiss. She's glaring equally threatening looks at all present. The menfolk cower. Everyone retires, and no further disturbances are heard on Kenwick Drive that night.

· · ·

In the summer Dad likes to lay out on the front porch if he's not asleep in his chair. He's out there now, lounging comfortably and watching TV. The chaise lounge is positioned so that he can lay on his stomach with a good view of the TV that's on in the living room.

I keep watch. After he falls asleep, I close the porch door on him. It's fun! He wakes up and swings the door open with his left arm to watch some more TV. I wait for his eyelids to droop and shut the door again. After a few iterations of this routine he gets pissed off, but since he's often in a bad mood anyway and Terry says I'm a brat, well, that's his problem. Dad keeps falling asleep and I keep closing the door.

I'm too quick on the draw this time. One of his eyelids pops open, just like the time he caught Leo trying to put a hairnet on his skull early in the morning. He doesn't say anything, but his ice-cold one-eyed Cyclops gaze sends a chill down my spine. I release my grip from the doorknob and back away. I don't go anywhere near the porch for the rest of the night. When Dad finally gets up, I give him a wide berth to avoid any confrontations.

• • •

CHAPTER TWELVE

CREEPY CRAWLIES

It's Saturday afternoon in the fall of fourth grade—a great day for playing tackle football up at Webster School. Just like baseball, pick-up football games draw onlookers that soon become players. It doesn't matter if the kids don't know each other. The opposition fields a blond haired kid who's the second biggest player, right behind Leo. I'm the fastest kid on either team. If I get a step on anybody I'm gone, forget it, touchdown!

The game's getting a rough edge to it. The blond stranger gets some good tackles on me but sees my back more often than he wants to. I zip past him with blazing speed for another score. The Kenwick team's lead grows to an embarrassing spread and his rage grows in proportion. It's further amplified by repeated slam tackles from Leo, and David's trash talking.

David and I both know there's something about Leo that can incite rage. The blond kid's about to join our club, recipient of yet another textbook tackle:

a) Drive shoulder into ball carrier's midsection
b) Wrap arms
c) Lift ball carrier off ground onto shoulders
d) Slam ball carrier into ground, knock wind out

Blondie's dazed and highly agitated from experiencing another perfect tackle, the lopsided score, and David's endless taunting. He snaps and flies at Leo in a rage, ignorant of the risks to his health. Leo thwarts his attack. Blondie finds himself face down in the grass with Leo on his back, introducing him to the insect world of Webster School. As usual, Leo shows little emotion, which only makes the kid madder after Leo lets him get up. David taunts Blondie about the grass stains on his face, goading him to go after Leo again. He does. I'm watching it all unfold in slow motion. I shake my head, because I know what's coming.

The cycle repeats twice more. Both times ending with a certain face better acquainted with grass, dirt, and bugs. The blond kid's friends drag him away, still raging, tears leaving streaks down both sides of his grass-stained face.

The Kenwick team carries the day convincingly.

• • •

It looks like it's going to be an early winter, after a brief fall. Mr. Vinciguerra's driving us to school this morning and we're freezing in the back seat of his car, waiting for it to warm up. There's a glaze of ice on the windshield. The defroster's blowing at full blast, but the cold air coming out fogs the windows and just makes the ice thicker. Mr. V. can't find an ice scraper, so he carves small viewing holes around the car with a credit card. He gets in and wipes away the fog with his handkerchief, but only what's within reach of the driver's seat. He puts the car in gear. I wonder how he can see where he's going. Somehow we make it the few blocks up Kenwick to Grant Boulevard. Finally the heat kicks in, clearing the glass and relieving my fears of Mr. V. driving blind.

My teacher this year is a short, round-faced person of Hawaiian descent. She's an aspiring protégé of Sr.

Mary Walter—her name alone sounds the alarm. Whenever a nun's name begins Sr. Mary followed by a male name, it's a bad sign.

Like her mentor, she carries a wooden pointer and she's not shy about using it. Nothing escapes her attention. You pay the price for violations of the rules and wrong answers. But she's gained notoriety for a unique deterrent reserved for bad little children who don't know how to control their hands. Getting your hands into something you weren't supposed to or touching classmates often results in painful consequences.

I'll show you what happens to people who don't know what to do with their hands!

The *showing you* part involves her closing the upward-opening desktop onto the backs of our hands, and then sitting down on top of it. Everybody's glad she's a small person. I'm convinced there must be parts of Hawaii that you don't read about in the tourist magazines.

We exact a revenge of sorts in her classroom, though unbeknownst to her. Once again I find myself unsupervised in a classroom with John of radiator fame. This time we're accompanied by a couple of other boys. John can't control his unsupervised happiness. Being something of an exhibitionist, he drops his drawers for a spontaneous rendition of the theme song from *The Beverly Hillbillies*. He provides the banjo music with his voice and enthusiastically strums his flapping dink to the rhythm. For the bass notes, he stretches himself out with one hand and strums his balls with the other. It's hilarious. We drop our pants to join the chorus. We're having a riot but have to complete the performance quickly. Nobody wants to find out what happens to boys who don't know what to do with their dinks.

•••

Inclement weather finds us in the basement of the Vinciguerras' house. We're getting bored, stuck inside. Bobby suggests a weightlifting competition, and his brothers David and Little Pauly like the idea. Big brother Louie's there and he's bored himself, so he joins us. Happy for a temporary distraction, he shows us how to handle the bar and correctly hoist it over our heads.

Bobby assigns himself the job of adding weight to the bar. We take turns lifting. Little Pauly's a hardened competitor and puts in a respectful showing, but he's younger and lighter and gets eliminated early. To my surprise, I'm pretty good at weightlifting. I strain less than Bobby and David against the increasing weight. At the end, I'm declared the winner but encouraged to try ten more pounds.

Bobby adds the weight, I clean the bar up to my chest, jerk it over my head for a regulation lift, and hope that Bobby and David are jealous. I'm new to weightlifting and setting records, and a little embarrassed by all the attention, so I sit down on the couch in between Bobby and Pauly. That's fine. But I cross my legs, which doesn't go unnoticed by Big Louie. I've seen that look of disgust on his face before, when I told the Carapella brothers that I couldn't fight because I had to stay clean before dinner. He's giving me another big dose of disgust now, leaning his face down close to mine to impart wisdom.

You don't lift weights and cross your legs, Lugi.

I uncross my legs and suddenly remember important chores that require my immediate attention at home. I slink out the door, having experienced both the thrill of victory and the agony of defeat within the same minute—another Kenwick record.

•••

Winter of fourth grade passes without any major accidents and all of the same pleasures—Christmas, sledding, and snowball fights. The Science Club returns to action in the spring and, with the flowers in bloom, bug hunts again consume much of our time.

Several neighbors put great labor into their flower gardens and repeatedly warn us away when we're seen approaching with empty jars and butterfly nets in hand. Bugs, bees, and butterflies seem to be attracted to their most prized flowers, and we often extract blooms along with the bugs. We make sure to carry jars big enough to fit their largest flowers, much to the displeasure of Kenwick Drive gardeners.

George and Mary, both single and brother and sister, live next door to Joey, up the street from us. They're our parents' age, avid gardeners, and boast the best tulip patch on the street. The bees love the tulips. In a demonstration of bravery, I show everyone how to catch one without a jar. With Mary watching in horror, I carefully close the petals of one of her prize tulips around a bee with one hand, neatly removing the flower from its stem with the other. She stands aghast. I nonchalantly walk past her, lightly swinging my arm, closed fingertips on tulip with captured bee inside. The maneuver impresses the boys and they try it for themselves.

Then Mary tells George and they're both outside yelling at us.

The Science Club needs the tulip garden for another reason, too. We're performing experiments on the destructive powers of firecrackers. Tulips are the best thing we can find to hold the firecrackers upright. The petals grip, making it easier (and safer) to light our powder. They also provide measurable before-and-after effects, easily recorded for scientific studies. We schedule testing to coincide with times that George isn't home. Mary

becomes an unwilling witness to more than one exploding tulip.

Joey wants to see what happens if we put a jar over a
firecracker. Since he's the one with the firecrackers, he
gets to do all the experiments he wants. We place the
firecracker on his paved driveway and after lighting it,
put the glass jar on top. We all step back quickly. The
firecracker explodes. We watch the jar launch into the
air and crash back to earth in Joey's driveway, spraying
broken glass everywhere. It's not easy to clean up, but
we take heart, knowing that we played an important role
to advance the cause of science.

Other firecracker experiments include paper air-
planes, but sometimes the firecrackers fall out or the
planes land before exploding. That, plus the hazards of a
lit firecracker in close proximity to your head makes
Mary's tulips a much safer alternative for all concerned.
Still, it's hard to beat a midair detonation with the plane
going up in flames before it crash lands.

Living in close proximity to the Science Club proves
catastrophic for George and Mary's tulip garden. Between our bee hunts and experiments in physics, they're
left with a stem garden amidst scant tulips. They alert
Joey's mother to our crimes and she admonishes us. But
we don't much care. Club rules clearly state that irate
mothers remain the sole concern of individual members—providing, of course, that she doesn't pick up the
phone. So far it's Joey's problem.

Springtime provides the Science Club with a new
nocturnal activity—catching night crawlers. Tonight
we're allowed to catch worms at Joey's house. We water
the lawn after dinner and wait for it to get dark. It's fun
being outside at night with our flashlights, filling jars
with long, fat worms. The club's entirely focused on
looking down, walking softly trying not scare worms

back into their holes... when George jumps out from behind a bush. He's plotted an ambush. When we step
close to his hiding place he suddenly emerges with his
arms raised, screaming a loud, terrifying **YEEE-
AAAHHH!!!**

His scheme achieves the intended effect. Several
high-pitched screams from the Science Club fill the air in
concert, along with the drum of running feet and the
squelchy plop! of worm jars emptying onto the ground.
We're all pretty mad at George for scaring us like that,
and for all those worms that got away. But we're madder
still because he can't stop laughing.

George secures a sweet revenge, and retires inside to
tell Mary all about it. The escaping worms are pleased,
as well.

Touché!

• • •

Our interest in things that crawl isn't limited to insects. Somehow Leo and I convince our parents to buy
us a pair of chameleons. The lizards are an instant hit
with the Science Club. We all gather around to watch
them eat. Leo catches flies in his butterfly net and carefully removes their wings, taking care to keep them alive.
He drops them into the chameleon tank. It's thrilling to
watch our lizards stalk, capture, and devour their wing-
less prey.

Leo's the brains of our group. He expands the wing-
less fly feeding to benefit the spiders living in our
backyard. He calls the spiders his pets, and enjoys feeding them. The boys heartily agree. Soon everybody's
catching flies, eager to pull off their wings and throw
them into a spider web. Spider feeding always includes
somebody mimicking the high-pitched *Help Meeeeee!!*
from the movie, *The Fly*. Our pet spiders make short

work of cocooning the flies we lay at their table, and grow large from constant feeding.

After a couple months the lizard novelty wears off. Mom notices our lack of interest. She never liked the idea of a lizard tank on her mini-kitchen table down cellar in the first place, and she's tired of reminding us to feed them. Another week goes by. She rekindles our interest by telling us that they're dead. She's half right—one of them's on death's door, still clinging to life, but the other one's a corpse. The look on Leo's face tells me that he shares my remorse about the lizard death camp we created. Efforts to save the survivor fail and he soon expires too... or so we think.

To relieve our guilty consciences we place him in a small tin container—the trappings of a proper burial. The skeletal remains of his companion are pretty cool, though, joining our collection in the garage.

Leo says a few words, and we inter the coffined remains in our backyard, right next to Nicky's garage. Fellow club members become incensed upon hearing of the lizards' demise, especially for missing the funeral. We decide to dig him up for a do-over.

I disinter the remains for viewing. We're all startled when the corpse starts to twitch. The lizard's tremors send electric vibrations up my arm. I drop the casket with its occupant to the ground and jump back a few feet. We cautiously approach for a better look, never having encountered a lizard zombie before. He's still twitching, and I feel even worse for having first starved him and then subjecting him to a premature burial. We're at odds as to what to do next. Nicky suggests that we rub his body with holy water. If that doesn't help him, nothing will.

I run into the house to retrieve a small vial of holy water, praying it's not too late to save our tortured, former best friend. We're a Catholic family, so naturally we keep several vials on hand—it doesn't take long to find one. We apply the holy water, the lizard appears to rally... and we've just witnessed a miracle.

A few minutes later, he croaks for good. We lay his body to rest again, this time with the pomp and ceremony befitting his former station in life.

Boys will be boys, and also being scientists, we're compelled to defile his grave. We disturb the sleep of the dead many times to study his transition into skeletal remains. And boy, for one small lizard he sure does stink.

• • •

It's highly unusual for us to play indoors on a nice day, but today's an exception. We're deep into a marathon game of Monopoly on the Savastanos' back porch. The contest grows intense, fueled by the number of participants, an even distribution of property and cash, and our highly competitive natures. The game reaches a point where monopolies start to appear, but there's still valuable properties on the market and trade discussions commence. As negotiations reach fever pitch, the dinner bell rings and the game is halted. Everybody's determined to play on to the bitter end. We agree to continue after dinner. We're all skilled at how to eat and run, so this shouldn't take long.

Leo and I suffer in agony through the longest dinner of our lives. Dad's in rare form as the Table Monitor. We both want to choke him, even if it takes all four of our hands to fit around his neck. Or does he even have one? Sometimes I wonder.

After an eternity we're released, and hurriedly make our back way to Nicky's porch to finish the game. We're the last to arrive. We find the mood much changed. Unhappy facial expressions and angry tones of voice provide clues, but a quick glance at the board tells us why. In our absence Nicky has acquired new monopolies, the remaining railroads, and has even built hotels. To remain in business, the *bank* must take a loan from Nicky. His egregious, newfound wealth includes most of the orange five-hundred-dollar bills.

We're all mad at Nicky. He handles it well and weathers the storm, calmly insisting that he's not responsible for our memory problems. Mrs. Savastano puts an end to our bickering, which has grown louder than she's willing to put up with. The situation becomes dangerous when cracks appear in Nicky's cool demeanor. Nobody wants to push him too far.

We dejectedly give up the game and file out, leaving Nicky alone with the Monopoly board. I keep it to myself, but it's my fervent desire that he step in a big pile of Lassie's poop. Then walk all over the checkerboard tiles on their back porch.

• • •

We never play basketball for fun in the Vinciguerras' driveway. It doesn't matter whether we're playing P-I-G, around the world, nine-hole, or team competition. We all play to win, with taunting and gloating allowed.

Today it's a two-on-two grudge match, Leo and David against me and Bobby—the two older brothers against the two younger. David calls their team the Kenwick Drivers. With attitude and expletives, he predicts a lopsided ass kicking. Bobby and I eagerly accept the challenge. If they're the Kenwick Drivers, then we're the Driving Young Bloods.

Game on.

Much to the dismay of the elder Drivers, Bobby's a force, despite being the youngest. I make a few lucky shots, and the Young Bloods take game one. In game two

Bobby and I switch so that now he's guarding Leo and I'm guarding David.

It's unfortunate for Bobby.

Leo's dribbling the ball and slowly backs his way in toward the basket while I guard David farther out near the foul line. Suddenly, Bobby utters a despairing,

Ohhhhh!

He stops guarding Leo, who turns around and makes an easy layup. David cheers. I'm confused. I make my over to Bobby to see what's wrong and walk headfirst into an invisible wall of stench, recently inside of my brother. I share a room with him, so I know all too well what just happened to Bobby.

Leo's a team player, though. He waves a cautionary hand at David, halting his approach toward the basket and the toxic cloud. He's a sportsman, too, and agrees to a time out to clear the air on the court, and for Bobby to regain his senses. Bobby tells me that we have to switch back or he's not playing anymore. David hears him and says, *If you quit, you lose.*

Game over.

•••

At the end of the summer after fourth grade I'm old enough to play little league football for the first time. Leo, Nicky, Joey, and David already play. We gather in Nicky's basement to discuss the impending start of football season. I've never played with more equipment than a football helmet, and start to ask questions about the other gear that's worn. The guys describe the different kinds of shoulder pads, plastic mouth guards, cleats, and various pads worn below the waist. In line with our developing fascination with human sexuality, the equipment topic turns to the protective cup. I fail to consider the risk, and blurt out fateful words.

Yeah, and Nicky's cup is shaped like a boner!

Everybody bursts out laughing. Everybody that is, except for Nicky.

I turn to leave, with echoes of laughter still ringing. He confronts me at the bottom of the cellar stairs. With one foot on the bottom step I'm turned halfway around by a fuming Nicky. He delivers several telling blows to my gut that best Leo's reaction to meatballs and sauce in his face. I don't know how many blows I absorb, but I'm pretty sure that he held me up for the last one.

I'm lying prostrate on the open staircase, having a view of below hitherto unseen. Several large ants scurry by. After a long minute I regain limb function and begin the ascent on all fours, still gasping for breath.

I can honestly say that I have an out of body experience—from up near the ceiling, I watch myself claw my way towards home.

Some people just can't take a joke.

•••

CHAPTER THIRTEEN

THE TALK

There's an old expression about learning it on the street corner. It's an accurate description of how I abruptly learn the facts of life. My brother Leo leads the conspiracy, and all of the older boys are in on it.

It's an otherwise normal summer day on Kenwick Drive. After finishing my lunch, I head out the front door to find the next adventure. To my surprise, adventure awaits *me*—right on the front sidewalk.

Leo, Nicky, Joey, and David huddle in a group, straddling their stingray bicycles. The bikes all pretty much look the same—long banana seats and high, chopper style handlebars—except that Joey rides a Schwinn five-speed and we're all jealous. Nicky's bike sports a sissy bar in the back and it makes his bike look cool. It's called a sissy bar because it keeps the back passenger from falling off—the principal safety flaw of the two-person banana seat. Annoying passengers find themselves jettisoned by frustrated drivers with great regularity. Nobody wears a safety helmet.

They've arranged their bikes in a circle, the riders eagerly leaning in and speaking in hushed tones, with serious looks on their faces. The conversation gains in intensity after I'm spotted at the door. It ends abruptly at my approach. My three friends look intensely at Leo, waiting for him to say something. After a moment's hesitation he finally speaks. I find eight eyeballs fastened on me in great anticipation.

So, ah, Looge, he begins. *What are you doing?*

Nothing, I reply, wondering if my fly is open or something.

Err, ah, let's ride down to the corner, he says.

It has an awkward, forced ring to it.

Okay, I just need to grab my bike out back, I reply, and run to get it.

With each step toward the backyard, my suspicion grows that something fishy's going on. And what's with him calling me Looge, anyway... almost with affection, too? It couldn't mean that he really likes me. Nobody's talking while we peddle down the street. The boys don't even look at me, making my uneasiness grow. When we arrive at the corner, it's my turn to ask Leo his own question.

So Leo, what are we doing?

He looks uncomfortable yet determined, and after another pause with everybody's eyes bulging out at him, he continues.

Looge, do you know where babies come from?

There he goes with the Looge again, and why is everybody staring at *me* now, I wonder. I'm feeling perplexed by the recent activities, but relieved at the same time. It's a safe enough question with an obvious answer.

It's a miracle, I reply with confidence.

I thought everybody knew that! Besides, that's what Mom told me when I asked her, so it must be true.

I look around at the long faces. My heart begins to sink during the silence that follows. Leo's the one being eyeballed now—another warning sign. My suspicions kick back into high gear. There's lots of neck snapping going on. It's a good thing we're young, or somebody might get whiplash. The suspense grows and Leo finds his voice again.

Err, ah, Looge, he resumes.

I'm thinking, one more Looge and he's going to catch a good one in the gut.

You ever seen those dogs up the street?

I start to answer and pause after a small light starts to turn on in my head. I reply in a cracked voice with a long, animated one-word answer.

Yeh-Eehhh-sssSS...??!!

There's three phases to my answer.

a) Acknowledgement that I'd seen the dogs.
b) A leading question, yes?
c) Great revelation—especially after Leo wiggles his eyebrows up and down (hint, hint).

Nicky, Joey, and David remain silent, taking it all in and pondering the part they played in the exploitation of a harmless child.

I scream and peddle home as fast as my legs can take me, distraught with visions of Dad giving Mom *the business.*

*He's doing **that** to **my** Mother?*

I think differently about my parents now. My life is forever changed.

• • •

Up until now I've only imagined what certain parts of the female anatomy look like, but that too is about to change, courtesy of Nicky and his older brother Joe's girly pictures. Nicky is two grades ahead of me in school and his brother Joe is several years older still. Putting these two facts together, it's easy to understand why Nicky knows way more than me about the birds and the bees. Whether he inspired Leo to straighten me out I'll never know, but the dog analogy was one hundred percent Leo.

Standing in the middle of the Savastano driveway in broad daylight, Nicky's telling us about explicit pictures that he found in Joe's secret hiding place. Nicky likes to find his brother's hiding places, even at the risk of a severe beating if Joe finds out. And he always does. Nicky's about as good at covering his tracks as Joe is at hiding things. Each discovery provides the neighborhood with a concert of assault noises and Nicky's bloodcurdling screams. Mr. Savastano puts a halt to the beatings if he's home. Then, an eerie silence follows.

After getting wind that pictures like this exist and that he's recently seen them, we badger Nicky to produce the evidence.

Where'd you get the pictures, Nicky?

You didn't buy 'em, did you?

Having his own paper route, Nicky's a self-made man and a free spender.

Nah, found 'em in Joe's room.

Where?

Joe hid 'em in his sock drawer.

That's not a great hiding place, Nicky, Leo reasons.

Why not? There's lots of socks covering 'em up. You'd never see 'em unless you dug through all the socks.

We exchange puzzled looks. He describes what he's seen. According to Nicky, the pictures show every part of the female anatomy in great detail, and some depict excited men having their way with naked women. It's all too much. The goading intensifies.

Sneak us up to Joe's room, Nicky—it won't take long!

No way, he'll kill me if he finds out.

But he always finds out, Nicky!

C'mon, let's sneak upstairs!

No! I'll go and get 'em, just wait here. I swear you guys act like you've never seen girly pictures before!

Well, duh.

He disappears behind the garage door. Now I have *two* reasons to be jealous of Nicky. Not only does he have a garage in the *front* of his house, he also has access to girly magazines, albeit cleverly hidden in Joe's sock drawer.

He soon emerges, photos in hand, with no pretense of concealment to any measurable degree.

I gotta put 'em back before I get caught, he says.

It's obvious that if we're going to look at printed filth, it's got to be right here, right now, or never. I'm beginning to see why Joe catches Nicky whenever he finds

Joe's secret hiding places. Sometimes Nicky doesn't put the stuff back at all, opting to hide the booty in his own room. The beatings intensify whenever his crimes escalate from trespass to theft.

We make the obvious choice. I take a quick glance over my shoulder to make sure that Mom's not watching us. My eyes behold images that I could only, well, imagine. Or maybe not even that. Nicky's right about the graphic nature of the pictures. They resolve once and for all any lingering mystery about what grown women look like without their clothes on.

The tandem pictures, however, prove difficult for my recently innocent but inquiring mind to process. I gawk in wonder at the size difference between some of the men. It's very confusing. The biggest man in the room's actually the short, skinny guy—how on earth could he ever fit *that* inside a woman? And I can't understand why they'd even want to let him try. It must hurt... doesn't it? Now I'm feeling sorry for those poor girls.

All right, that's enough, Nicky says, and snatches the pictures from our hands. My mind's racing now. Before he disappears again behind the garage door, I dreamily remind him to put the pictures back in Joe's sock drawer, and to bury 'em deep.

• • •

It takes me a couple of weeks to get over the constant visions of what's hiding at the bottom of Joe's sock drawer. I'm having nightmares about the short, skinny guy chasing naked, screaming women up and down Kenwick Drive. There's abundant analytical DNA in my gene pool and combined with curiosity it's a fatal combination. There's only one true test, so I start looking for something to take measurements with. I check the junk drawer in the kitchen for a ruler or something, but come away empty-handed. Not to worry though, we always keep a yard stick over the top of the back door.

I live to regret it.

After making sure that nobody's watching, I grab the yardstick, head into the bathroom, and lock the door behind me.

In my heart I already know that I'm no short, skinny guy, but the results disappoint me nonetheless. I unlock the door to return the cursed yardstick to its spot, and hear noises coming from the entire family in the room outside. Not wanting to get caught coming out of the bathroom with a yardstick I put it down next to the toilet, planning to return for it later, unobserved.

I exit the bathroom and promptly forget all about it.

A little while later Mom reminds me. She's standing outside the bathroom with the evidence in hand.

Who had the yardstick in the bathroom?

Leo and Terry quickly answer in the negative. I begin to dissolve into the cracks of the hardwood floor in the dining room, where Mom's demanding an answer. The family stares at me in disbelief, anxious for my reply. I pray for a miracle that it all blows over. My bad luck is running in spades, because it's Saturday and Dad's home. Not only can he not be my alibi—his ears perk up. After hearing the dialogue, he joins the others in staring at me in the dining room. My prayers go unanswered. Mom's unrelenting.

Lugi, did you put the yardstick in the bathroom?

I hate it when she asks questions that she already knows the answers to.

No, Mom, I reply, still praying for the miracle but thankful that I'm not measuring now, because the results would be even worse.

Don't lie to me, Mister! What were you doing in the bathroom with the yardstick?

Nothing, I automatically respond, my belief in miracles fading by the second.

The pressure mounts and I begin to stammer.

Well... I... uh...

Well, what? Speak up, I'm waiting!

My miracle arrives in the form of a witty answer, and playing the safety card, too!

Well, I, ah, measured the window in there to make sure that it's big enough for me to get out in case there's a fire.

My clever response only makes everybody laugh at me, even Dad. And he's an unhappy camper unless there's a clambake.

Mom's not buying it.

Right, she says mockingly.

Next time you need to measure anything in there, use a six-inch ruler instead—because they don't make anything smaller.

Coup de grace delivered.

The day's measuring up to be another long one ahead.

•••

With all of the measurements happening on Kenwick Drive, my parents realize that perhaps it's time for them to have *the talk* with me. After a few days, Mom gets up her courage. Visibly distressed, she's the first to broach the subject.

Lugi, I'm supposed to talk to you about these things, you know...

Aw, Mom, I reproach her, trying to put on the airs of a man of the world. *You don't have to! I already know all about that stuff!*

She's dying to drop the subject and jumps at her first chance.

Okay, but you can ask me about it if you want to... because I'm supposed to talk to you about these things, you know?

Okay, Mom!

She returns to her housework, the weight of the world off her shoulders. She's walking away and I almost call her back to ask if you're supposed to go pee first. What else to expect from Captain Yardstick, man of the world?

But I don't.

Not long after releasing Mom from her maternal obligations, I'm walking past Dad seated in his favorite chair... and he raises the subject, too. He's reading the newspaper while he speaks, his face hidden behind it.

Louis... he begins. Dad's still the only one who calls me Louis.

You know all about that stuff, don't you? He's talking in a deadpan voice and obviously still reading. Dad's a skilled multi-tasker.

Yes, Dad, I reply, stopping to answer.

Good!

I stand there and wait for him to say something else. After he doesn't, I throw in a *Thanks, Dad,* and go about my business. We never speak of it again. I admire his efficiency.

•••

Mom's relieved to get off the hook so easily. That night we're allowed to play a game of touch football under the street lights in front of Joey's house. It's a real treat and, because it's a rarity, we put on our football helmets to enhance our fantasy of playing in a real NFL Monday Night Football game. The street lights and the sensation of night air rushing past the earholes in my helmet add excitement to the game. My team's winning, mostly because I'm the fastest kid on the field and nobody can catch me. Who says that fear doesn't have its advantages? I'm wearing my lucky New York Jets helmet, the same one that saved me in the go-cart fiasco. Life is oh, so good.

Two dogs break all protocol of spectator behavior and run onto the field, ending our fantasy.

Until this point they've kept to the grass, fitting in nicely with our illusion of NFL Monday Night Football. They're real spectators—who cares if they walk on four legs?

I'm ready to go out for another long bomb touchdown pass, right past Joey, who has no answers for my blazing speed, when a ruckus breaks out in the stands. The ball gets hiked. My first step takes on the entire weight of my body. Suddenly the fans rush onto the field in great excitement. The first dog's a near miss, but his pursuer scores a direct hit to my right knee and bends it the wrong way. The collision lights up the sky above me. I learn there's truth in the expression about *seeing stars*. The dog lets out a yelp but quickly continues in pursuit of his idiot friend. I later petition the league to ban beer from night games, but for now I'm down for the count.

Staying true to established medical procedure in NFL Monday Night Football, the player/medics take my helmet off. I'm grabbing my knee in pain, but the helmet removal comes first, those are the rules. They look me over. I'm told that the dog injured my knee but I'll be okay eventually. I'd strangle the medic if not for the pain, and I'm carried off on my shield, as it were. Next, I'm loaded onto the back of the banana seat on Leo's bike and hold on for him to drive me home.

During all the commotion my lucky Jets helmet gets left behind.

Before we depart, I hear Joey complaining that he'll have to walk home if he rides my bike back for me, and Leo stalls to contemplate how to ride one bike while steering another. My heartfelt moans must strike a chord, however. He decides to take me home first and solve the bike problem later.

It's after hours at the doctor's office when the injury occurs, so I'm compelled to survive until the next morning. Mom gives me some aspirin for the pain and puts me to bed with extra pillows around my damaged knee. It hurts to move my leg but eventually I drift off to sleep.

Mom brings me to the Doctor in the morning. He feels all around my leg and knee, continually asking me, *Does this hurt?*

It doesn't tickle.

After he completes the examination, I'm told that I sprained my knee, and shown how to figure eight an ace bandage around it. I'm equipped with a pair of crutches. He tells me to stay off it for a week and for Mom to bring me back then. The look on his face and the high-pitched tone of his voice make me laugh after I tell him what happened.

You were hit by a dog?

Yes!

And looking at Mom, I ask her to tell Leo to go up the street and look for my helmet.

• • •

CHAPTER FOURTEEN

STANDING UP

There's something about the woods that attracts boys of all ages and compels them to build a fort. A large wooded area seven blocks away from my front door calls to us. It's located next to the Syracuse China factory on Court Street, within sight of school boys from St. Daniel's and Lyncourt Schools alike.

We talk it over in our club. It's a no-brainer for us to go and build a fort there. Our chief architect and carpenter Nicky takes charge without objection, because he's the one with the tools—with or without his Dad's permission. Summer vacation is waning, so the sooner we start, the better. The next morning we put our plan into action.

The club assembles on our bikes in front of my house, destination woods and future fort. Everybody's here: Nicky, Leo, David, Bobby, Pauly, Joey, Ricky, and yours truly. Nicky carries a box containing the cutting tools, and the rest of us divvy up hammers and nails to bring. Highly excited and in great anticipation of adventure, we're all pretty anxious to reach our destination. Too much so, in fact.

We reach Court Street, a thoroughfare busy enough for two lanes of traffic in both directions. Our excitement builds to a frenzy, with the woods in sight just across the street. Our leader can't contain himself. While crossing the street at great speed, he drops his box of cutting tools. It's then that we discover he's been carrying an assortment of large kitchen knives, now scattered all over the middle of Court Street in broad daylight.

Fortunately traffic is light. We jump off our bikes, desirous to retrieve the knives quickly while not attracting attention. It's a precarious situation for passing motorists, who face the challenge of avoiding boys, bikes, and large kitchen knives right in the middle of Court Street. Nicky rallies us to gather the knives and we make it across with nobody getting run over.

Our destination within reach, we turn off Court Street to follow a dirt path leading into the woods. After it becomes impractical to go further on our bikes, we leave them by the path and continue on foot. Now that we're cutting our way through the overgrowth, I understand why Nicky chose to pack all of those knives. They're sure handy, even if they're not machetes.

I find it exhilarating, chopping my way through the jungle. I want to get a safari hat for the next expedition. We decide on a good spot to build our fort—it has natural, thick growth around the perimeter, but is somewhat cleared in the middle. We commence cutting branches and soon wish that our leader had packed a saw or two. Cutting tree branches with dull kitchen knives produces more blisters than lumber.

Our grandiose plans require big branches, but after an hour of work there's only one branch to show for it. We're all sweating profusely. Being scientists with a resident architect in our group, we scale back our design and manage to cut a few decent-sized but much smaller branches. Soon, a few get nailed to trees growing close to each other, providing a glimpse of the final product. But at this pace it's going to take months to complete. Leo, our club know-it-all, has a brainstorm.

Let's look for fallen branches lying around, and use them instead!

Sometimes the kid has good ideas, even though you wish you'd heard it from somebody else. Using his strategy, progress improves dramatically. We call it a day after running out of nails.

• • •

Today's the first day of fifth grade, and it's off to a bad start. My teacher, Sr. Clare, should have been named Sr. Mary Something-or-Other, because then at least we'd have been warned. She looks like a Sr. Mary Charles to me. She's another first-time teacher for the Visconti kids, so once again there's no history to rely on. On day one I detect there's something off about her—my Bad Nun radar picks her up and locks in for tracking.

After I get home, Mom asks me about my first day at school.

How'd you like your new teacher, Lugi?

I don't like her!

Why not?

I don't know, there's just something about her...

Oh, you're not even giving her a chance—it's just the first day!

I know, but...

Unfortunately, my instincts prove correct. I inherited my first impression sensor from Mom. It's a double-edged sword, more bad than good. Leads to a lot of jumping to wrong conclusions, and all that.

Sister Clare likes to give homework—lots and lots of it. After filling the blackboard with another lengthy assignment (in every subject), she writes the word **ONLY** in big bold letters and underlines it twice. During an extensive homework session one night after dinner, Mom grows tired of listening to me whining. I'm seated at the dining room table and she comes over to investigate.

Oh, this isn't so much!

She mistakes the assignment sheet for a completed assignment, and returns to the couch in the next room. I quickly correct the oversight.

Mom, that's not the homework I did, that's everything that we have to do!

What do you mean? That can't be right—let me see that again!

She snatches the lengthy assignment sheet from the table and her jaw drops.

You must have copied it down wrong. This can't be right!

*It is, Mom! I copied it down exactly word for word! And, oh yeah, she wrote the word **ONLY** at the end, like she always does, and underlined it twice!*

I don't believe you.

She did, Mom! Call somebody else's mother if you don't believe me!

I will! I'm going to call Mrs. Jackson—and if you're wrong, you're going to get it for making me call her!

The clouds immediately begin to part in the home-work dining room, for two reasons.

First, my story will be verified.

Second, of all the mothers in my class, she's calling Mrs. Jackson.

Mrs. Jackson, the mother of Mary Beth Jackson, born on the same day as me. Mary Beth Jackson, the woman I've loved every day of the four long years since Kindergarten.

One day last year, in the midst of the end-of-the-day bustle, I was talking with her and a few other kids, and she blurted out that she loved me. This announcement made her blush after she said it—that, and her cousin Eileen asking her, *What did you say? What did you say?* in a stunned, excited voice.

Meanwhile, I, Captain Yardstick himself, melted into the floor and missed my chance.

Mrs. Jackson attests to the lengthy assignment. My eavesdropping leaves me wondering if I didn't write down all of it. She confirms my claims about the double-underlined **ONLY** at the end. She says that she doesn't think Mary Beth will finish, as she'd been at it for two hours already and it's getting late. She adds that Mary Beth is in tears. The call ends.

Ah, if only I were there to take her in my arms and comfort her! Another chance missed.

Mom hangs up the phone. She's visibly disturbed.

We'll see about this!

Now she's looking through the junk drawer in the kitchen for the phone book so she can make a call to the convent, the nuns' residence. I watch in silence, still dreaming of consoling Mary Beth. But I begin to feel the first pangs of anxiety at the thought of Mom talking on the phone with Sr. Clare.

She dials the convent number and in a moment they're connected.

Sister Clare, this is Mrs. Visconti. I just want to ask you one thing, Sister. **Are you crazy?**

Mom doesn't wait for an answer and continues.

Do you really think that fifth grade children could complete all this work in one night? Because they can't!

The short, one-sided conversation continues but the tempo only leaves time for *Yes, Mrs. Visconti*-type answers. After hanging up, Mom says that Sr. Clare said to finish what you can and everything will be all right.

The next day I walk into the classroom on eggshells, not knowing what kind of reaction I'll get from Sr. Clare... but to my relief, she doesn't retaliate. At least not today. My worry radar's still scanning, though.

Sr. Clare's in a league of her own when it comes to intimidation. I wouldn't argue if somebody told me that Sr. Mary Walter fears her. My sensing that something's off with her right from day one seems to make her especially dangerous. More than a few times a terrified fifth grade class witnesses her assaults on unfortunate schoolmates.

Her favorite technique is the two handed full-body shake. She secures her victim by planting her fingernails into their biceps, then shakes them back and forth into her terrifying face while uttering threats in a voice from hell. The girls aren't exempt from this maneuver, either. Usually the most extreme physical reprimands are reserved for the boys, but Sr. Clare believes in equal opportunity.

After watching an especially violent encounter—and seeing biceps with broken skin and fingernail marks—I vow that I'll never endure such an outrage.

Wrong!

Our class goes on a field trip to the Burnet Park zoo. Being in close proximity to wild animals, the group naturally begins to act like them. The vast majority of kids, even the girls, behave badly, and Sr. Clare, along with the homeroom mothers, has her hands full. The next day begins with a lecture about our misdeeds. We're informed that each and every one of us must write a personal letter of apology to the homeroom mothers, including specific examples of the crimes we're repenting for.

For once in my life, I honestly did not misbehave on the day in question. My sense of fair play cries out in protest, albeit silently. Everyone immediately gathers up paper and pens from inside their desks and begins writing. Everyone except me, that is. I'm struggling with the injustice of it all, and I don't feel that I owe anyone an apology—especially not a detailed, written one at that.

Pens and pencils start moving. Sister Clare directs us to put our assignments on her desk after we're finished. In a short time, my classmates begin the procession up and down the aisles with their letters of remorse. The girls finish first, of course. Sr. Clare grows impatient, reiterating that she expects a letter of apology *from everyone*.

She sees the blank paper on my desk and repeats her demand, glaring directly into my eyes in a challenging manner. Stubborn and stupid, I try to wait her out and see if I can get one past her. She gives the class a break for recess and I think I'm in the clear. Whew!

Wrong again.

I'm still missing one letter, Mr. Visconti, and you're not going out for recess until I have it!

I sit there another five minutes watching my classmates having a good old time. She shows no sign of retreat. I finally cave in, scribble a hasty apology, and after depositing it on her desk I join my classmates to enjoy what's left of recess.

My one liner, *We are sorry for what we did,* doesn't cut it with Sr. Clare. She calls me back to her desk. She's fuming.

I said to be specific and to take personal responsibility!

I make a fatal blunder, attempting a direct rebuttal.

I didn't do anything wrong, Sister!

Now she's blowing her stack. My errant lips seal my fate.

... And we have rights, too!

I had no idea she could move so fast. Before I know it my biceps are locked in the claw hold, my head, face, and body propelled back and forth into the vision of a demon from hell shrieking at me.

RIGHTS? RIGHTS? YOU THINK YOU HAVE RIGHTS?

My latest experience with public humiliation ends with me being shoved backwards over a chair and onto the floor.

She retires in victory to her desk at the head of the class. Several shocked classmates come to my aid while I tremble on the floor. Worst of all, there's no stopping the tears.

It's okay, Louis, one says.

You'll be all right, she's mean, whispers another.

Boy, are you stupid, remarks a third.

Glancing around the room from the floor I discover that most kids look away before our eyes meet. Then I see Mary Beth casting a sorrowful look right into my red-eyed, tear stained face.

My life is over.

This is the final straw. I start muttering that I'm going to take off. My classmate Mark both hears and believes me, because he goes and locks the door. Is he trying to help me, or piling it on? Either way, I'm not far behind him. Casting a final look of defiance toward Sr. Clare, I unlock the deadbolt and throw the door open with a crash. I engage the blazing speed the good Lord blessed me with and take off down the hall that connects with the school cafeteria.

Emerging from the cafeteria door into daylight and fresh air on the sidewalk outside I'm confused, distraught, and still sniffling. Now what? I never bothered to plan an escape route along with my act of defiance. But even through my confusion I manage to concoct a plan that doesn't take me past the front of the school and the principal's office. My brain's overtaxed by the confrontation with Sr. Clare. I'm convinced that the principal and every priest and nun at Assumption have instantly become aware of what just happened. Furthermore, they've alerted the custodial staff, using a secret phone line. A bad little boy has escaped, and he must be captured and brought to justice immediately.

There's only one safe harbor open to a runaway fugitive, and it's four blocks away.

Gramma's house.

I still want to avoid the front of the school, but my stealthy detour takes me only a quarter block away from the place I want to avoid, and at an intersection with a street light to boot.

Nobody ever told me that runaway fugitives don't have to wait for the light to turn green or look both ways before crossing. My escape is halted by a traffic light. I can't run up Pond Street to the protection of Gramma, the woman I used to avoid at all costs, until the light changes.

I'm staring up at the light, hyperventilating and anticipating the hands of unseen pursuers clamping down hard on my shoulders to drag me back to the principal's office—most likely my chief adversary herself. The light turns green. I take to my heels, not stopping to look back until I reach the top of the hill, halfway to safety. I cautiously turn around, expecting to see an approaching cavalry of nuns, priests, and janitors in hot pursuit, but I'm the only soul in sight. I turn back around and walk the remaining two blocks to safety.

A few steps from her door, I realize that Gramma may not be home. Then what? I can hide out in her garage or walk another two miles home, giving the posse ample time to subdue me.

Please be home, Gramma!

I put my hand on the doorknob... and it turns! Gramma's more than a little surprised to see me. She listens intently while I recount my misadventure. She utters, *Black Devils!*—words she occasionally uses to describe the nuns. She picks up the phone to tell my mom a good one and hangs up in short order. She addresses me in her lovable Italian Grandmother accent.

You a Mother is, ah, coming here to get you.

Gramma hugs me and starts to fix me something to eat—the cure for every ailment known to mankind.

I love you, Gramma. And Gram, I'm sorry for not letting you walk me home from Kindergarten.

Mom quickly makes the two-mile trip from Kenwick Drive. Gramma fixes her a plate. We all eat together while I repeat my tale. Gramma remarks again about the Black Devils.

It slowly dawns on me that Mom's more incensed over the mistreatment by Sr. Clare than she is about me running out of school. It's a confusing day indeed.

We finish our solemn meal. We kiss Gramma goodbye, and don't talk during the drive home.

I can tell that Mom's deep in thought so I remain silent. Once home, and after allowing herself time to think, she digs the phone book out of the junk drawer again and dials the convent number. This time she asks to speak with the principal. Being a lifelong communicant of the Church and an alumna of the school, Mom's well connected with both the sisters and the clergy, and the principal knows this.

Hello, Sister, this is Mrs. Visconti. Uh, Sister... are you missing any little boys today?

I'm surprised by Mom's unemotional demeanor. Is this really *my* Mother talking? It's Mom's intention to let the principal do the explaining. It's an effective tactic. I listen in great apprehension from the next room and hear an *Okay, thank you, goodbye* much sooner than expected.

Mom doesn't say anything more about it until Dad comes home. She tells him of my day's adventures. According to Mom, the principal apologetically stated that she'd heard about what happened, and acknowledged

Who ya gonna call?
Nun-Busters!

that they were having problems with this particular nun. And she asked Mom if she would *please* let her handle the situation. Mom did—and after the school year ended, Sr. Clare no longer taught at Assumption. She may have left the convent, too.

All these years Gramma and Mom have both loved me more than I ever knew. How they supported me today proved it.

•••

After my escape from school, things cool down both inside and outside the classroom rather suddenly. Winter comes on almost overnight, and Sr. Clare appears as anxious as I am to forge a truce. I buckle down to my studies and abandon my self-appointed leadership of the protest movement. Safer to keep my head down and stay out of trouble. Who cares if the other boys now expect great things from me?

The early snow brings sledding, the joys of Christmas, snowball fights, and more daring adventures in our snow-filled backyard. If you step out of our back door, you're standing on a sidewalk that runs along the back of the house. To the left of the door, the sidewalk ends abruptly in a five foot, cliff-like drop into the backyard. We call it, well, the Cliff.

When there's deep snow, we run down the back sidewalk to see who can jump the farthest off the Cliff into our backyard. Sometimes we pile up snow on the steps and use it as a sledding hill. It works pretty well, but with the Wrobbel's steep hill next door, we only use it if we've annoyed our way out of permission to play in their backyard. Strangely, hitting their house with snowballs can get us banned.

Although I'm the bravest one in our club, I don't have exclusive rights to being the dumbest. One day Leo decides to try sledding directly off the Cliff. He chooses a plastic sled for his endeavor. Sled in hand, he gets a running start on the back sidewalk. Just as he reaches the edge of the Cliff, he drops the sled to the sidewalk and jumps on. But instead of propelling out into the yard, he dives straight down in a crash, bashing his head against the side of the Cliff. I'm watching in slow motion. He reminds me of the Coyote in a Road Runner cartoon—all we need now is for the anvil to fall on his head.

As he's lying there I suggest that on his next run he add cinderblocks, just like we did with the go-cart in the street. My advice clears his head. He's up the stairs in an instant, throwing me off the cliff.

Was it something I said?

• • •

Kids on Kenwick make snowmen just like kids do in every other snowy part of the world. Nicky's a kid, and he made a snowman. Unfortunately for the neighborhood, the arrival of this particular snowman coincides with our recent fascination with sexuality. Leo and I decide that Nicky's snowman requires some alterations.

To be fair to Leo, it's my idea initially—I make the first modification to the snowman. There's good packing snow, and by four o'clock the sun's setting. In no time I've given the snowman a member of much larger proportion than the ones I'd seen in the girly pictures Nicky showed us in his driveway last summer. Short, skinny guys around the globe are now shamed. To make no mistake about what the snowman's packing, I sculpt a conical, helmet-like head to his manhood, and place a couple of decent-sized snowballs beneath.

Leo watches and laughs, but doesn't want to be left out of the fun. A short time later the snowman grows two large man-boobs, complete with ice nipples. For all I know, we've created the world's first transgendered snowman.

I'm just starting to carve the crack into the snowman's ass when Mom calls us inside. Lucky for us, she doesn't have a good angle on the snowman or our pornographic sculpture. Being the two dopes that we are, Leo and I go inside, leaving the snow-thing alone in the dark.

The next day is Sunday. The Savastanos pile into their station wagon to go to church. Mr. Savastano's backing out of the driveway, but stops abruptly upon catching sight of Nicky's altered snowman on his front lawn. Father and son exit the car and remove the frozen abominations. I'm sure that Nicky has some explaining to do, but he pleads his case successfully because we don't hear any screams.

Our phone rings. I hear Nicky's voice on the phone talking to Leo.

Ah, Leo— I know it was you that did that to the snowman!

Leo mumbles a denial. I sense that he's genuinely worried for a change. This is great—I hope it lasts! The phone call ends quickly because they're running late for church. We do our best to avoid Nicky and his Dad for weeks afterward.

I never believed it until now, but going to Assumption rather than Lyncourt actually does have its advantages.

•••

I've witnessed and partaken in many fights by the spring of fifth grade. Throughout all of them, there's one cardinal rule strictly observed by all combatants: *No hitting in the face.* The rule doesn't apply to the big kids in junior high and the really big kids in high school, but for kids of my age group in the vicinity of Kenwick Drive, it's carved in stone. Even during the epic battles of David versus Ricky, not one blow was directed above the shoulders. Leo rubbed that blond kid's face into the dirt at Webster School to his heart's content—but he never punched it. In all of the poundings that I took from Terry, Leo, and Nicky, my looks were left intact. Pretty much everything else is fair game except the obvious restrictions on private parts. But no hitting in the face!

That's all about to change.

It's a big world out there beyond Kenwick Drive, with kids who see things differently and play by other rules. Unbeknownst to me, one of them sits across the aisle in my fifth grade classroom.

A disaster occurs after an otherwise normal day in school. I've kept the peace with Sr. Clare and feel safe enough there. But lately there's been a lot of fighting among the boys, I'm not sure why. One or two of them are regulars, and they're working their way through the class roster, notching their belts along the way. I notice, too, that once a person is vanquished, they're bullied afterward, which is worse. I know from experience what it's like to get beat up—but then it's over with. The emotional aftermath of bullying hurts more than a physical beating. As I'm about to find out for myself.

I'm one of the last boys challenged to a fight after school. I'm not overly surprised or concerned when it happens. After all, I'm a veteran combatant. I've survived beatings at the hands of assailants older and larger than any of my classmates in the fifth grade. No problem.

School lets out and I find myself outside, ready to square off against my antagonist. I don't know why we're fighting, but I answer the bell after being challenged just because. He eyes me with disdain and throws his books on the sidewalk. I smile and do the same, following pre-fight protocol. The familiar script unfolds, with several iterations of back and forth shoves.

And then it happens.

Whack! Right cross to the jaw, no questions asked. I'm not hurt, but rather incredibly stunned by this outrageous violation of the rules. I begin to verbally correct him about his breach of childhood law when another salvo lands from the other direction.

Whack! Left hook to the other side of the button. This kid can hit with both hands.

I'm standing there taking punches to the face, my hyper-analytic brain trying to process at warp speed. But no information comes out of the system except for sound of fear bells clanging. The onlookers watch in disbelief. I'm hearing it from the crowd.

Ooh! That one must have hurt!

Aren't you going to hit him back?

What's wrong with you?

Still standing and relatively unhurt, two things finally occur to me. One, hitting in the face is allowed in this venue, and two, he's doing it. I'm left but one alternative in the age-old struggle of fight or flight—I pick up my books and run like hell. Mom's picking us up from school today, and mercifully her car is just around the corner in the parking lot. My blazing speed should save the day. My adversary senses fear. In hot pursuit, he delivers a final parting blow for good measure.

I jump in the back seat, slamming and locking the door in great haste. Leo, Terry, and Mom don't know what just happened. I don't say anything during the ride home. That last punch really hurt. Upon arriving home I look at myself in the mirror. My heart sinks at the sight of a black eye—an advertisement of shame, if there ever was one, in all the colors of the rainbow.

There's no hiding it. Soon everybody in the house knows. What can I say? What can I do? I wish there was a hole to hide in.

Dad questions me at dinner. His lack of empathy only makes it worse. I think he's ashamed of me. Once again, it's Mom to the rescue in yet another fifth grade misadventure. She picks me up from school for the next few days, and even pulls up by the door to make sure I'm okay. Leo and Terry don't like having to wait in the parking lot and it's all very humiliating. But I welcome Mom's support with a flood of relief.

The ensuing weeks in school, especially until the badge of humiliation fades from my eye, is without a doubt the worst time in my life. Word of my demise travels quickly and my classmates mark me a coward. I endure the mistreatment the best I can. Going to a Catholic school, I seek comfort in Jesus... and He hears me.

During what's become a routine public display of dominance, my adversary starts to talk me down. Only this time I don't just take it quietly. A spark of courage

suddenly emerges from the scant remains of my back-
bone. It's not unlike what happened to the Grinch after
his sled began to slide down the side of Mount Crumpet.
The fifth grade holds its breath. I step forward. I look
him in the eye and, nose-to-nose with this bully, with
great deliberation, I find my voice.

Why don't you leave me alone?

Everyone, especially me, expects an onslaught... but
nothing happens.

He moves on to easier targets. I practice deep
breathing techniques, envisioning puffy clouds and
ocean waves.

That night before I fall asleep I get down on my
knees and thank the good Lord that it's almost summer,
and that I'll be attending a different school in the fall.

You know, getting a chance to start over is a beautiful thing!

•••

FOR LITTLE PAULY
(November 23, 1963—June 6, 2015)

This book is dedicated to my childhood neighbor and dear friend Paul Vinciguerra. As the youngest of the Kenwick kids, Little Pauly made sure he was never left out of anything we got ourselves into. He had to try harder than everyone else to keep up, and he

Pauly and Aunt Anne Marie

always did. His never-ending smile was his trademark, no matter what the circumstances.

He was around sixteen when he became Uncle Pauly, just saying it was a shock—he was always Little Pauly to me. After that I never called him anything but Uncle Pauly, and although we joked about it I confess that I never completely got over it, even into my fifties.

I was visiting my grown children in Florida in June of 2015 when my brother called to tell me the sad news about Pauly leaving us. I had planned to meet him for lunch the following week to discuss an idea for our church, and now I wish that I hadn't kept rescheduling. Another lesson learned the hard way. Pauly taught me to keep my cool, try hard, keep smiling, and lastly not to put things off. This book is the result of his final lesson.

Pauly combined two admirable qualities: a can-do work ethic and a winning smile. They took him far. While he may not be remembered as being great, he was always good—something that's even better and harder to do. He was a good brother, a good son, a good husband, a good dad, a good uncle, a good worker, and a good friend.

Thanks for everything, Pauly.

•••

ACKNOWLEDGMENTS

Without the support and encouragement of my family and friends, this book would have remained a dream. Constant badgering and requests for feedback must have tried your patience, so thanks for hanging in there with me. Some of the best stories would have been missed without my brother Leo, who sparked my memory and witnessed (or perpetrated) most of it.

I want to acknowledge all of my neighbors growing up on Kenwick Drive, especially my childhood friends. This is as much your story as it is mine. I sincerely thank you for all the wonderful memories. Writing this book was a labor of love, and I had no intention to ridicule or embarrass anyone other than myself.

Thanks very much to my fantastic editor, Maria De Angelis, for putting wings on the project and guiding me across the finish line. Kudos to Chuck Schiele for his help with the photo graphics, and especially for the work in progress on the audio version. Thanks also to Jon Dufort for pinch-hitting in the bottom of the 9th and batting in the winning runs – too many to mention.

Last, but not least, I'd like to thank my beautiful wife, Sue, without whom I'd never get much of anything done. You're the best part of my life, and I love you.

•••

ABOUT THE AUTHOR

Lugi Visconti is a comedy writer with a past drenched in red sauce. He's lived most of his life, minus a short stint in the Navy, happily married in the Syracuse, NY area. After thirty-three years in the corporate world he's found time for writing comedy, embarrassing himself, and impromptu visits to his far-flung grandchildren. Lugi is writing a sequel to *Kenwick Drive* that picks up where the Science Club left off and has plans for a series of humorous, illustrated books for children.

•••

55129753R00127

Made in the USA
Lexington, KY
11 September 2016